SEMI-PRIVATE ROOMS

Jim Sanderson

SEMI-PRIVATE ROOMS

PIG IRON PRESS

Youngstown, Ohio

Winner of the 1992
Kenneth Patchen Competition
Pig Iron Press
Publisher: Jim Villani
Judge: Al Young

ISBN 0-917530-34-9

Library of Congress Catalog Card Number: 94-67559

Published in Youngstown, Ohio

Pig Iron Press
P.O. Box 237
Youngstown, Ohio 44501

For My Parents

Margie & Sandy

Funded Through
Ohio Arts Council

Acknowledgments

"A Pink House." *Cimarron Review* 57 (October 1981).
"Ladies' Man." *Cimarron Review* 101 (October 1992).
"The Commerce Street Bridge." *Descant* Fall-Winter 1984-85; reprinted in *New Growth II: Contemporary Short Stories by Texas Writers*, Ed. Mark Busby. San Antonio: Corona, 1993.
"Bit by the Metal" as "Drags." *Concho River Review* Fall 1989.
"Stripping." *Ellipsis* 1.3 (1989-90).
"The Case Against Billy Feeler." *New Growth: Contemporary Short Stories by Texas Writers*, Ed. Lyman Grant. San Antonio: Corona, 1989.
"Potential." *New Mexico Humanities Review* Fall 1983.
"A Life in Venice." *New Texas*. Denton: Center for Texas Studies, U. of North Texas, 1991.
"Boomtimes." *Re: Arts & Letters* 17.2 (Fall 1991).
"Viejito Loco." *The Vanderbilt Street Review* 2 (Spring 1981).

Table of Contents

FOREWORD

The ideas of a narrative feasting on the Southwest, a *Semi-Private Rooms* of the prairie, the desert, the frontier townscapes, and a Kenneth Patchen Competition, a tribute to a voice of the culturally disenfranchised poets, artists, social visionaries, and laborers on all fronts, are ideas fated to find each other, to meet, to mate. I don't suppose I would ever have thought about Odessa, would ever have read Jim Sanderson if not for a competition, a winning of it by Jim, a perceptive decision by Al Young, judge of the First Annual Kenneth Patchen Competition, to award the prize to Jim Sanderson and *Semi-Private Rooms*. I think that Jim, I, the Competition, and Pig Iron Press have gained something herein; with pride I put the winner of the first Kenneth Patchen Competition in your hands, for your read.

The stories that constitute *Semi-Private Rooms* range through arid geographical and psychological landscape. The narratives are not specifically West Texas, although the attitude of Texas, in its purest form, is present herein. Texas oil towns are places where nobody wants to be. The populace transient, the landscape ugly, people develop a tough attitude toward their world, fatalistic and ironic. Jim supposes that even though the source of these conversations is the West, is Texas, is the greater Odessa region generally, he has been hearing these stories all of his life, no matter where he was. These tales, in final assessment, are Jim's attempt to put some meat on to the bones he has heard people picking.

Consider "Stripping," which launches the book. Lisa Tomlinson, or **Captain Hook's** "Angelica," is an Oklahoma City stripper, past her prime, eager for a change of life that includes dancing. In "Bit by the Metal," with his wife hospitalized in Austin, Bo Fralix oscillates between an affair with a professional woman and hallucinatory memories of his grandfather's impact on shaping sexual compulsiveness. Bailey Waller gives up his sales job at a strip plaza Odessa car dealership in "Potential," to attempt to regain lost youthful football glory by becoming coach of a boys' military academy team.

In "The Case against Billy Feeler," Dawn Cox has an affair with Billy, a banker, refuses to run off to Mexico with him after spending the night in his Wagoneer, and then hears him shot down by the Midland Police inside a Town & Country convenience store. Monty Parker's buddy OD's in his Los Angeles apartment in "A Life in Venice," and the drifter -- smuggler -- hippy goes home to Monahans in search of abandoned parents, rejects them all over again. Bred in suburban Houston, married to a young professional in Fort Stockton, a first-time-pregnant housewife befriends Hispanic Elodia and her daughter, and joins the Junior League in "Boomtimes." "Ladies' Man" knows about certain Houston women; he can spot them, women who look better in their clothes than out of them; the first night together is mysterious, but a bit clumsy; the second, third nights are better, but there are problems attached to the pursuit of these women.

Illegal border crossing is traditional, a business; under "The Commerce Street Bridge" in San Antonio, the system may be threatened by the rise of the dope smuggling trade and its impulse to exploit established alien border crossing traffic. Sister Quinn, in the Big Bend area, ministers to rural border Mexican peasantry and wetbacks in "Ocotillo"; some say Sister Quinn can turn into an owl, just like the souls of the dead. Julius, a *nigger*, takes up residence in the property shack in "A Pink House," in a Southwest Louisiana bayou, cleans up the yard, undertakes repairs, paints the shack pink, while *Missus* leaves food on the porch of the house she lives alone in. Old man Casoose, Mexican wino, wanders the streets by day, sits his nights in West Texas jails playing his harmonica and dreaming about the old times in "Viejito Loco."

Jim attempts to poetically render rural Texas meanness and desperation in the present sequence of tales. Not all Texas psyche is mean, desperate, or disconnected. Let me close with the acknowledgments and thank-yous that demonstrate Texas virtue and support, that enable Jim and me to offer this collection to you for judgment. Craft and sensibility are the anchors that Jim, as writer, depends ever so much upon. He thanks his guides in developing that craft, his mentors, especially Gordon Weaver. Additionally, for sensibility, Jim thanks his drinking buddies, male and female, including Barry Phillips and Truett Hilliard. Lastly, a thank-you is tendered to Jim's friend, fellow writer, and teacher Terry Dalrymple, and his family, for all their help and good company.

Pig Iron Press has its own acknowledgments to tender. The creation of a juried Kenneth Patchen Competition required immense support and assistance. First, I extend a sincere thank-you to Al Young for his contribution, his patience, and his judgment. In Al's estimation, the "adventurous, dramatic, funny, sad" stories that shape *Semi-Private Rooms* "deal knowingly and compassionately" with Southwestern tradition. Kenneth Patchen, he observes, who wrote about the working class psyche, would have "responded sympathetically" to stories like "Ocotillo" or "Viejito Loco," and would have "cried and laughed" over "Bit by the Metal" and "Stripping."

The organizing and executing of this competition required the dogged persistence of a handful of colleagues. I thank Bill Mullane, who agreed early on that the proposed competition was a fitting tribute to Kenneth Patchen. Bill arranged to seat Al Young as judge of the first contest. I thank the Ohio Arts Council and Bob Fox for both encouragement and financial support. I thank novelist Jack Remick for organizing the screening committee that pooled and ranked manuscript entries. I thank my pool of interns and volunteers who labored with me to craft and design the finished book, that labored so fastidiously through numerous copy-edits, typing procedure, proofreadings, and page designing. Lastly, and perhaps most sincerely of all, I thank Miriam Patchen, who has been a most courageous supporter of my modest efforts to honor Kenneth Patchen with prior projects and with the new Competition.

I close with a global thank-you to all those courageous supporters I cite herein. I can never pay them enough for their contributions. The gold is in the narratives that pick up in the following pages. Enter and enjoy.

Jim Villani

STRIPPING

"And now, the legs and the face you've seen in the Big Country Mobile Home Commercials," the announcer growled into the microphone. "One fine lady. Captain Hook gives you . . . Ms. Angelica." **Captain Hook's** had an announcer, a stage with a runway, a carpeted dressing room, clean restrooms, and a long bar that curved around two walls. It was Oklahoma City's best titty bar. A stripper at Captain Hook's didn't have to rely upon tips and table dances to make a living.

Lisa, who allowed Bobby Cox, the owner of Captain Hook's, to call her Angelica, walked out onto the stage, started tapping her fingers, pointed her feet out, then back in toward each other. She wore a G-string, a tight, low-cut black vest, a bow tie, high heels, a black derby, and white gloves. Lisa danced only with her hands and feet to a selection from the score of *All That Jazz*. Her Bob Fosse number. "Meat's on the table," she heard from the audience. Bobby Cox still liked her, no matter what, and he told his manager, Leonard, to allow her three of her own numbers a night.

Lisa turned sideways to her audience: grubby guys in T-shirts and jeans, just off work. She dipped her knees, pulled her derby low over her forehead, and shook her other gloved hand as she raised it over her head. Then, she dropped her head, let the wrist of her raised hand go limp, and strutted down the runway.

"Lick some nips," she heard a man shout. At the end of the runway, she turned, unbuttoned her vest, shrugged her shoulders to let the vest fall. If she was going to work as a nude dancer, she was going to be nude. Lisa saw no sense in teasing them during the first dance, then shedding her top in the second. She only wanted her props. She worked in Oklahoma because, although the state had crazy liquor laws, it didn't require pasties like most other states. When an Oklahoma titty bar said "all nude," it meant it.

Lisa raised the derby up over her eyes; then she briefly closed her eyes, listened to the rhythm, and started to dance. The whistling and catcalling, which usually didn't stop until later in the night when the men got drunk or horny, halted as the men watched Lisa's dance. It was a cat-like dance that she had choreographed years before for a Dallas Community Theater production of *The Pajama Game*. Sometimes, if she could find suitable music, she used the staccato dance she had made up when she dyed her hair and played Anita for a touring company of *West Side Story*. She had been Cassie in *A Chorus Line* on a tour of Tulsa, Dallas, St. Louis, and Louisville. Had Cassie's number not lasted so long, and thus kept other dancers from taking their turns, she would have done it at Captain Hook's. Lisa didn't dance much anymore except when she stripped. Occasionally, she would audition for a part or get a recital at Oklahoma City University or the University of Oklahoma. She might have gotten more parts or teaching jobs at the two schools if fewer people knew what she did for a living.

But, in a titty bar, she could steal the time to strut her stuff.

These men with scarred knuckles and brown teeth remained silent and watched her closely because they were seeing something different and could sense that it was special. Lisa hugged the pole in the middle of the stage and wrapped a leg around it and looked at the men. She appreciated them just as they, she knew, were beginning to appreciate her dance as much as her tits and ass. She unwound herself from the pole with Fosse's smooth, hydraulic moves. Dancing Fosse tired her because of its stretching and meticulousness, but Fosse fit a stripper's routine.

The music stopped, and Lisa let her head drop and bowed. The men hesitantly applauded; none whistled. They didn't know how to react to what they had just seen. Bobby Cox had told her that men expected themselves to act a certain way in a titty bar, and despite beauty or the dance itself, confused men lessened profits. Lisa didn't give a damn about Bobby Cox's profits. Later tonight, they wouldn't be able to distinguish her own dance from the dances of the other strippers. Their eyes would glaze over; they would smile as they gazed up at Lisa, and they would stuff bills in her G-string. Now, even these men knew they had seen something special. Sometimes, after seeing her dances, a man would return just to watch Lisa.

Her next dance in this set was what Bobby Cox and all the other titty bar owners wanted. Lisa gyrated. She didn't twirl her tits, but she bent over, peeked at the men from between her legs, crossed her arms, stuck them between her legs, and rubbed the backs of her thighs and the cheeks of her butt. Even when she danced for Bobby, she found new moves and new body angles that men would think were sexy. She combined moves that other strippers hadn't even thought of. With this dance, she got a few tips. After the men stuck the folded dollars into her G-string, Lisa bent over, smelled the beer, tobacco, and spicy lunches on their breaths, and kissed them.

When Lisa finished with her dance, she grabbed her vest, ran to the women's restroom, and bent over the sink. She tried to breathe slowly and resist the urge to suck in all she could. From her days tap dancing in elementary school, through ballet in junior high, and modern dance in college, she had hyperventilated. She could feel the smoke wafting in her lungs. During her performances, she gulped whatever air she could, but the stale air in topless bars is filled with smoke. Several doctors had told her to stay out of these places, but she resorted to catching what fresh breath she could in the women's restrooms.

She ran some water and splashed it on her face. She went to the automatic hand dryer and pressed the large knob that sent the hot air out. She squatted to hold her head under the air nozzle, then her face, then her chest. The machine seemed to create air, even if hot, and dried the sweat. Strippers always had colds.

"Jesus, you need to take it easier," Lisa heard from the row of stalls. She looked toward them and saw the auditioning stripper coming out of a stall. She had a G-string, high-top pink tennis shoes, a punk haircut that looked like a rooster's comb, and a push-up bra on her young, firm, sagless body. She had a tattoo of a butterfly on her left shoulder. A long scar, like a tattoo, probably from a Caesarean, ran down from her belly button to her G-string.

"If it's easy, it's no good," Lisa said.

The young girl, around twenty, Lisa guessed, stuck out her hand and said, "I'm Monica."

Lisa pulled herself from under the hand dryer, nodded her head, but didn't shake the young girl's hand. "Bobby and Leonard like that name," Lisa said. "What's your real name?" But, before the youngster could answer, the changing temperatures in Lisa's body made her feel just a bit sick in her stomach; then a lump, which she knew was a cramp, knotted in her hamstring. She cried out, bit her bottom lip to stop the scream, and grabbed at the back of her thigh. She tried to hold the cramp where it was and keep it from working its way up into her hip.

"Can I help? Jesus," the youngster said. Gritting her teeth, knowing what she had to do, Lisa limped to the sink and lifted her cramping leg to it. She touched her forehead to her knee, kept her leg muscles taut.

Bent over her straightened leg, the sink groaning with her weight, Lisa heard the door to the *ladies* room open. She looked over her shoulder to see Carol. Carol had a size 42 bust, and those grapefruit breasts had made her lots of tips until, after three husbands and two kids, her hips and belly also started getting big. She was one of those women destined to turn to flab after she gave birth. She was now ***retired*** from dancing and waited tables because Bobby Cox replaced her with a younger, thinner girl. "Are you okay?" she asked Lisa.

"Yeah," Lisa said and straightened up. Carol's gossamer negligee pressed so tight against her tits and hips that it looked like a mist around her. She looked naked but airbrushed, like the *Playboy* centerfolds. Lisa knew about centerfolds. Years ago, between tours, she had gotten two pictorials, but not ***the*** centerfold for *Penthouse*. She had gotten airbrushed so that she looked twenty. Lisa swung her head to look at the new stripper. The youngster asked, "Do you go through this every night?"

"Yeah," Carol said, with a hint of malice before Lisa could answer.

"I saw your first dance. It was really good, even beautiful, but I don't get it."

Lisa brought her leg down from the sink and turned

to face the younger girl. "It's real dancing," Carol said.

Lisa turned, smiled at Carol, then smiled at the new girl. "It's variations on a theme. Movements."

"But, I mean it doesn't make any money. You can't get tips that way. What's it get you?"

Lisa hung her head, then brought it up to look at this girl. She had started feeling maternal toward the younger ones. "Respect," Lisa said.

The youngster smiled and walked past Lisa and Carol. When she got to the women's room door, she turned and said, "You can't eat respect. I got two kids to feed since my old man ran out." The young girl walked out the door and left it swaying on its hinges.

"Why are they always so tight-assed their first night?" Carol said. Carol's heart tattoos were on her inner thighs. Her mother had been a stripper and, as she worked her way up from dives to Captain Hook's, Carol had danced several times with her mother, who was working her way down. Lisa started slipping back into her vest. Then Carol said, "She's your new competition."

At quitting time, Leonard asked Lisa to come into his office. Before he took over managing Captain Hook's, Leonard was a cop. Bobby Cox liked to have ex-somethings – cops, teachers, businessmen, grocery store clerks – run his titty bars. He figured that, as an ex-cop, Leonard could protect his girls. Leonard kept his .45 in his office and a small .22 under the bar. The guns made Lisa nervous. To her, Leonard seemed like the type who was just too anxious to use them.

Leonard's office was behind the stage and next to the girls' dressing room. Rather than a door, he had a red drape. When Lisa saw the young auditioning stripper step out of Leonard's office, then look back in to blow him a kiss, she didn't wait to put on her street clothes. She let the young stripper leave; then she pulled the red drape open and saw Leonard with his hand resting on top of the screen of his new IBM computer, his nose about two inches from the screen. His hand slowly formed a fist. He said, "Goddamn it." Bobby Cox had bought computers for all his titty bars to see how much liquor he sold and how much he needed to order. "Son of a bitch," Leonard said, pulling back his hand as if to punch the computer screen. His tattoo, a screaming eagle with *U.S. 8th Army* written underneath it, was on his left forearm.

"Leonard," Lisa said and sat in the chair across from him.

"Sons of bitches," Leonard said and jerked his head toward the computer. He turned his chair toward her. Leonard couldn't keep his eyes from drifting down, then rising up as he soaked up the sight of Lisa's legs.

"It's late, Leonard. I'm hungry, tired," Lisa said. Leonard pushed his office chair toward Lisa, leaned back in it. He drummed his fingers next to the computer keyboard. When he hung his head, Lisa said, "Oh, shit. Shit. Where's Bobby?"

Leonard rolled his chair toward Lisa. "Now don't bother Bobby over this." He looked Lisa in the face but couldn't keep his eyes from moving down the V of her vest. Lisa knew that she should have gotten dressed. Leonard had worked in Bobby Cox's bars for nine years, but those years were not long enough for him to grow lackadaisical about strippers' bodies.

Lisa turned away from Leonard, scooted her wheeled chair toward the door, and pulled the red drape open. She could see across the dance floor to the bar. Sitting on a bar stool, his back to the bar, his elbows propped up on it, was Bobby Cox. Lisa felt a clammy palm on her knee and turned to see Leonard patting her knee. "You know, Lisa, I liked being a cop," Leonard said, and quit patting Lisa's knee, but lightly rubbed it. "But, I eventually had to quit."

Leonard's hand moved farther up Lisa's thigh.

Lisa pulled her leg out from under Leonard's hand, stood up, and said, "Your stupid analogy is bullshit." Lisa pushed the red drape aside and walked around the stage and to the bar. She stood in front of Bobby Cox with her hands on her hips. Bobby was a good-looking man with blonde hair and deep set blue eyes. His hand moved slowly and deliberately as he sipped his scotch.

"Now, Lisa," Bobby said and raised his glass to his mouth so what little light was in Captain Hook's reflected off his diamond pinky ring. His Porsche was parked outside. His button-down oxford cloth shirt was crisply starched and monogrammed on the pocket. He had on pleated wool-blend pants and black cowboy boots that might have cost as much as his Porsche. Bobby brought the glass down from his mouth. "Sit by me, Lisa," he said.

Lisa sat on the bar stool next to Bobby and squirmed from the plastic seat biting at her naked butt. She looked down the opposite end of the bar to see Carol pushing a Bissell. Carol would be trying to hear. Bobby downed his drink, and Lisa heard the clinking of his ice. He set the glass on the bar and jerked his head in his slow, calculated fashion, like a devious Robert Redford, saying, "Look at her." Lisa looked to see Carol. "It's all she's got."

"Don't patronize me, Bobby," Lisa said.

Bobby swivelled toward Lisa and laid one of his open palms across the top of her hand. "The point is that you have so much more than she does. You're obviously talented. But I can't make money running a talent show. I wish I could." Bobby patted Lisa's hand and moved closer toward her. "Your looks have stayed with you, and you're smart."

"I'm also a dancer."

Bobby smiled at her and said, "See? See how smart

you are? You have a fast mind. Hell, you could catch on twice as fast as numb nuts Leonard in there trying to figure out which computer key to push." Lisa stared at Bobby's forehead and looked at his blue eyes. He never looked at her breasts or thighs like Leonard. He touched his strippers, but not with clammy palms, just a warm cupped palm. Lisa saw from his expression that he would listen to her, whether she wanted to beg or threaten him, but that he would not let her dance again. "You need to go on. Time you gave up this kid's game."

"Okay, give me my pink slip," Lisa said and tried to slide off the bar stool, but the plastic held on to her, pulled her skin.

"Please. Not so fast," Bobby said, and slowly spun around, pulled her around with him until they were facing the bar. "I want you to manage a place for me," he said and stared into the mirror behind the bar. "Not pity. An honest chance. I think that you can make money for me."

When Lisa swivelled to look at him and sighed, "I don't want to be a businesswoman," Bobby turned toward her and put his cupped palm on her shoulder.

"We're all business people," Bobby said. He pulled his palm down, reached into his pocket, and brought out his rolled wad of bills. He took the rubber band off it and peeled off three hundreds and four fifties and handed them to Lisa. Lisa heard Carol's voice say, "Holy shit."

Bobby said, "This can be an advance for your new salary, or it can be your severance pay. And, if you ever need anything else . . . ."

Lisa gritted her teeth and jumped off the bar stool, nearly ripping the skin off her butt. She folded the money into her palm, smiled at Bobby, and said, "Like most people, you did the least you could do." She turned away from Bobby, went to the dressing room, slipped her jeans on over her G-string, pulled a sweatshirt over her head, stuck her arms into the sleeves of her Levi's jacket, and made it to her 280 Z in the parking lot before she started crying.

Lisa sat in an all-night coffee shop, drank iced tea, and ate a hamburger before she went home to her townhouse. It was the first home she had ever owned. The road shows and the tours never allowed her enough time or money to live anywhere but in small one-bedroom apartments. Stripping, commercials, a poster, the *Penthouse* photos, and her tours gave her enough money to buy the three-bedroom townhouse in a secure, northwest Oklahoma City subdivision.

Lisa felt reluctant to tell her white, middle-class neighbors how she made a living. She might have enjoyed the shock she would have given them. Instead, she told them half-truths about teaching aerobics at The Body Shop and occasionally teaching a week-long seminar on dance in the public junior highs. With the half-truth, the neighbors wondered where she got her money and why she stayed out late, but they were not curious in the way the truth might have prompted them to be.

Lisa flipped on her living room light, pulled off her high heels. She ground her feet into the soft carpet to let it massage her toes. She pulled off her jacket, sweatshirt, jeans, and, in her G-string, did her stretching exercises. Without her exercises, cramps, with all the creeping subversiveness of age, would form in her legs and move up into her hips.

While she stretched, she reached to the coffee table and spread out the mail in front of her. Bills. On the lamp stand was the bill from Mini-Maid, the company that had just cleaned her apartment. After stretching, Lisa went to her refrigerator and took several swallows out of a quart of milk. Her doctor had recommended milk for her slight calcium deficiency.

After she showered and brushed her teeth, she lay in her king-sized bed and flipped on her answering machine. She had gotten two calls from Fred Wemple, wanting a date for dinner. Fred was forty-four, divorced, and fighting twenty-five pounds in Lisa's aerobics class. She taught the hour-long class at noon three days a week. Most of her aging businessmen students with Baptist wives and spreading paunches had asked her out. None knew what she did for a living.

She had a message from Doris Rhodes at the Oklahoma Commission on the Arts and from Gerry Obermeyer at Midwest City Community College. Both would see her tomorrow. Lisa had been expecting Bobby to fire her and wanted to give herself some options before she started the slide down to the titty bars where she would have to rely on tips and table dances.

Gerry Obermeyer had National Junior College Athletic Association basketball championship rings on three of the fingers on his right hand. He wore his simple wedding ring on his left hand. His full head of hair, meticulously in place with mousse, looked like styrofoam. He sat in his glassed-in Athletic Director's office and looked out at Midwest City Community College's gym and recreation center's parking lot and the tall electric sign. The sign was a gift from Coca-Cola to Midwest City Community College's president for allowing Coke to have sole concession rights. It flashed out the time, the temperature, coming sporting events, and cheerful messages full of morality. Lisa had seen the messages before when she had driven by: "God gave me problems, but he also gave me shoulders" or "Discussion is an exchange of ideas; an argument is an exchange of ignorance."

"That is some sign," Lisa said, and Gerry Obermeyer swivelled his head and his chair to look at Lisa.

Obermeyer's chair creaked as he spoke: "Ms. Tomlinson, I can maybe offer you one class this summer, maybe two or three for the fall. But next spring, if Mrs. Hodgins retires, we will need a dance instructor."

Lisa sat with her hands in her lap. She rubbed her charcoal gray linen skirt and felt the collar of her Sunday school teacher's blouse rub her neck just under her chin. She looked out at the sign and read the message for the day as it flashed in back of Coach Obermeyer's head: "An error is an error once; a blunder is when it is repeated." Mrs. Hodgins probably liked that sign. Lisa knew Mrs. Hodgins. Back before the college got the new million-dollar gym with facilities that rivaled the work-out shops, back when Mrs. Hodgins was Acting Athletic Director at Midwest City Community College, Lisa had applied to teach dance. An ulcer and a slight stroke left Mrs. Hodgins with a limp, so Mrs. Hodgins, a one-time high school P.E. teacher, taught the dance classes at Midwest City Community College while leaning on a cane or sitting down. Once she retired, the college would probably name the building after Mrs. Hodgins. "What about these classes that I could teach part-time?"

Gerry Obermeyer put his elbows on his desk and studied Lisa's resume. "I can send references."

Coach Obermeyer ran one hand along the side of his head and left a dent in his hair. "Oh, no," Gerry Obermeyer said. "I don't know much about dancing, but this looks plenty impressive to me. All the shows you've done. A graduate degree from SMU." Gerry lifted his head up from the resume to look at Lisa. "What does M.F.A. stand for?"

"Master of Fine Arts, Coach Obermeyer," Lisa said. Earlier, when Lisa had introduced herself and called him Dr. Obermeyer, Coach Obermeyer had laughed and said that he had no doctorate. When she called him Mr. Obermeyer, Coach Obermeyer told Lisa just to call him *Coach*.

"Now, Ms. Tomlinson, what we need is somebody to teach these kids and occasional older ladies, bless their hearts, a little lifetime recreational activity. We have regular day-time classes, night classes, and special classes for senior citizens."

Lisa smiled against the tickling, yet hot semi-voluntary nerve in her heart and head that made her want to defend dance to Coach Obermeyer and to the students at Midwest City Community College. "Yes, yes, I realize that," she said.

"You know, we're just a little community college here and don't have much room for a curriculum with art-style dancing. We're not interested in anything fancy. We're just here to help folks."

Lisa smiled wider and said, "That has always been an aim of mine. We should demystify the arts. Take the name of art away and let them be entertainment or recreation."

Lisa then said to Coach Obermyer, as she had said to Bobby Cox when she applied to be a stripper at Captain Hook's without previous experience and at an age when most strippers retire, that dance, no matter in what form or for what reason, was still dance, and she could dance.

Coach Obermeyer propped his head up with his hand and squinted his eyes as he listened to Lisa. "Yeah, that's a good point," Coach Obermeyer said. "Can you teach country western dancing?"

The nerve twitching in her heart and head caused Lisa to choke slightly as she answered, but she raised her hand to her mouth, cleared her throat, and said, "Yes, I don't see why I couldn't."

"That's a popular course," Coach Obermeyer said.

"We could always use a course in that for our continuing education department."

Lisa closed her eyes, then quickly opened them and said as much to herself as to Coach Obermeyer, "I can do that."

"Well, Ms. Tomlinson," Coach Obermeyer said and stood. "I'm really impressed with you, and I'll give you a call or have my secretary write you a note."

"Is that all?" Lisa asked. "Is that all you want to know?"

"Oh, I can size up my people pretty fast. Comes from all the recruiting. I know how to get the right folks on my team," Coach Obermeyer said, and conspicuously held his right hand in front of Lisa and shook his ringed fingers. "You seem like you'd be a good community college educator. And I'm rarely wrong about people."

"Well, just one question, though, before I leave," Lisa said as she stood along with Coach Obermeyer. "Will I get the chance to dance myself?" Gerry Obermeyer cocked his head as he thought about Lisa's question. "Will I be able to do my own dancing?" Lisa rephrased her question.

"Well, well, no," Coach Obermeyer said and shook his head as if to make himself understand how to make his point. "You don't have to. You just teach dancing here. You don't have to do any dancing."

Lisa slowly nodded her head and smiled wider than she had. As Coach Obermeyer shook her hand, Lisa let herself ask another question. "Is there any dancing in the drama department?"

Coach Obermeyer again cocked his head and rubbed at his chin. "I don't know. I really don't know. This is the P.E. department. Takes all I have just to run it."

"Well, thank you for your time," Lisa said and turned away from Coach Obermeyer. When Coach Obermeyer pulled the door open for her, she asked,

"Where do you get the sayings for your sign?"

Coach Obermeyer smiled, "The company that donated that sign to us gave us a little book with those sayings in them. As Athletic Director, I get to choose which one to flash. That sign is really something, isn't it?"

"It certainly is," Lisa said, then added, "I think I'd enjoy working here." She turned away from Coach Obermeyer and walked through his door. As Lisa walked out the front door of the Midwest City gym and recreation center, the sign flashed out: "An error is an error once; a blunder is when it is repeated." Lisa got into her 280 Z, looked up at the sign, and thought about the impossibility of teaching dance as she understood it, not as Obermeyer understood it, to any student who would believe the sign's messages.

Lisa sat in a cramped conference room with reams of mimeograph paper stacked around the table. Doris Rhodes sat in front of the one window in the conference room and blocked Lisa's view of the Oklahoma State Capitol. To Lisa, the dome of the Oklahoma State Capitol was almost as ugly as the sign in front of Midwest City Community College's gym.

Doris Rhodes began to talk. "Look at this place. I can't get extra space. Got a shortage of computers and people. Working for this goddamn Republican give-a-shit-about-the-arts governor ain't worth a bucket of warm spit. You still want a job?"

Lisa had worked with Doris Rhodes before. Mrs. Rhodes, the director of the Oklahoma Commission on the Arts, used to regularly hire Lisa to be an artist in the schools around Oklahoma City. Working for Doris, she could dance with the kids.

Lisa wondered what interest Doris Rhodes could have in dance. A dancer knew that her hands or head lined up in a certain way could produce an aesthetically pleasing image. A dancer knew that she had to work with what she had, so a dancer had to be aware of herself: her age, her physique, her face, her limits, her talent. Doris, who was over six feet tall, stacked her hair on top of her head and made herself look seven feet tall. Around the office, Doris wore golden house slippers with curled toes because they were more comfortable than pumps or heels. She wore black, half-framed glasses. And she held herself always erect with her shoulders thrown back so that she looked like a drill sergeant. She was just as direct in her manner. "I can't send you out to the schools. The budget's gone to shit," Doris said.

Lisa could at least relax more here than in Coach Obermeyer's office. "I need a job, Doris." Doris didn't know what Lisa did as a living but probably suspected something that most typically employed Oklahomans would find disgusting.

"Why are you begging for a job from me? Look at your talent. Your qualifications. What are you having to hang around here for?"

Lisa knew why she was having to beg for a job from Obermeyer, or Doris Rhodes, or Bobby Cox. She told Doris Rhodes part of it. "I wasn't quite good enough. I should have taken more acting classes. My voice needed to be better."

"Well, hell," Doris said. "It's a shame." Lisa gave a shrug. "I can't give you a job dancing, but I can recommend you for this," Doris said and pushed a job description in front of Lisa. Lisa first saw the salary, $27,000 a year, then saw that the job was with the Commission on the Arts: awarding state grants, traveling to give advice across the state, appearing before the legislature to solicit funds. "You'd be one of my assistants," Doris said. "You're well-educated. You have a variety of experience. You look good. I look like shit. You're a woman. I think you could twist the balls of a lot of the old farts in this state."

Lisa read through the duties a second time, then looked at Mrs. Rhodes and asked, "Can I dance?"

"Honey, sometimes working for this office makes you want to dance; other times you feel like your feet are planted in cement." Then Doris turned into Lisa's mother. "Lisa, you need to give dancing up. But you can still be involved." And Rhodes shoved the application under Lisa's nose. "It's better than teaching for some son of a bitch like Gerry Obermeyer."

Lisa looked down at the experience section of the application. Lisa didn't want to leave a seven-year blank with only part-time teaching jobs accounting for the way she made a living. "Doris," Lisa said, "I'm a stripper. That's what I do for a living. I could do other things, but I like stripping. What happens when I put that down on this application?"

Doris folded her fingers together and looked over her half-frames at Lisa. "God, that is a shame. Pisses me off." Slowly, the corners of her mouth stretched back. "No shit," she said. "You really take your clothes off in front of men?"

"Yes, Doris. What happens when I put that down?"

"You put that down, you don't get a job because of the stodgy old farts who run this state," Doris said. Lisa stood up and let the application slide out of her fingers and float down toward Doris's desk.

"Wait," Doris said and caught the application before it landed. "Nothing says that you have to list stripping." Doris laughed. "I like the idea. A stripper working for the old bastards." Doris stood up and held the application out toward Lisa.

Lisa took a step toward Doris and grabbed the application. "It must give you some thrill to have such power over men. God, it would be fantastic."

Lisa had met many strippers who thought like Doris. "For me, there's no power. I just appreciate the dancing. You should come see me." Doris smiled, and Lisa knew that Doris wanted a better answer. Lisa could not give her the speech that she gave to Coach Obermeyer or to the community arts patrons, so she spoke while she thought. "Because I don't *have to beg* for money . . . because the men do appreciate me in their own weird way . . . . I like dancing in a titty bar better than dancing for rich, blue-haired, artless ladies who support and watch community dance troupes."

"You're a pretty smooth talker, honey. You'll make a good politician. You've got my vote." Doris held out her hand. Lisa hesitated, then shook her hand.

Fred Wemple talked about his faith. Lisa could feel the hair on his arm lightly tickling her bare shoulder as he tried to use his left hand to help him talk. She could not see him in her dark bedroom. She was glad. In the dark, lying on her back next to him, looking up at the rotating blades of her ceiling fan, she need not really talk to him. "I'm a Baptist, sure, but I don't agree with all the fundamentalism that's going on. I think any person can have a personal relationship with God. If a person says that it's okay for him to drink or dance, then I think that it's fine with God." Fred hesitated and waited for some comment from Lisa about her faith. "What do you believe in?" Fred asked after a pause.

Lisa believed that believing was not really different from feeling, but she knew better than to tell that to Fred. "I believe that I need to catch up on my sleep. It has been a really enjoyable date."

"Oh, oh, I'm sorry. I didn't realize. I've been babbling on and on and here you want me to go. I just didn't know."

"Please, just get dressed, Fred," Lisa said.

Fred was a squat man with a round chest and belly. Lisa watched his dark shape as he sat on the edge of her bed and looked over his shoulder at her. She smiled at him even though he probably could not see the smile. He stood and side-stepped, his back to her, so he wouldn't reveal any of his nasty parts to her. Lisa covered her face with her flat palms to keep from laughing. He was clumsy when he exercised, danced, fucked, or stepped into the legs of his pants. He was not aware of his body or of her body. Lisa lifted herself to a sitting position and watched Fred dressing, his back still to her. "Thank you for dinner, Fred," she said.

"Oh, it was my pleasure," Fred said. His pants and shirt on, Fred turned to face her. "This has been just a terrific evening for me. Since my wife and I split up, I've really just been so worried about meeting any really nice women . . . and . . . ."

"I'll walk you out, Fred," Lisa cut him off, folded the sheet down. Fred's form grew straight as he stared at Lisa. She walked to Fred, took his arm, and walked him through her dark house to the front door. She unlocked and slowly opened the door. The porch light lit Fred's face and, as Lisa knew, lit up her figure. The night air created a shiver on Lisa's shoulders, and it ran down her back and chest, forcing Lisa to hunch her shoulders and shake. Fred's eyes followed the shiver down Lisa's chest and stopped at her quivering breasts. His eyes quickly lifted so that she could see that he was looking only at her face. He leaned toward her to kiss her good night, then hesitated when she didn't lean forward, then pulled his face away from hers. He stuck out his hand to shake her hand, but Lisa crossed her hands over her breasts and hugged herself. "Good night, Fred," she said and closed the door when Fred smiled, as though saying goodbye.

Lisa turned away from the front door, pulled the afghan off her sofa, wrapped it around her chilled shoulders, walked to the refrigerator, and got her quart of milk. She walked back into her living room, sat in her easy chair, sipped her milk, and pulled her legs up onto the seat of her easy chair.

As she sipped milk and began to warm up, Lisa shrugged the afghan off her shoulders and traced the curve of her breast with her forefinger. She could feel the slight droop along with the goose bumps. She moved her hand down her side until she came to her hips and felt a pocket of fat. From the side of her hip, she moved her hand until she felt her female belly, a bulge below her waist. She was not in bad shape for a woman her age. She was not in bad shape for a P.E. instructor at Midwest City Community College. If Doris Rhodes was an example, she was in fantastic shape for a state bureaucrat. But she was not in good shape for a dancer. She was in fairly good shape for a stripper.

Lisa took a drink of milk. It was low-fat and tasted slightly sour. Lisa raised her knees until she could hug them. Fred had looked around her apartment when she invited him in, and he had commented that he didn't know that she made so much as an aerobics instructor. He had said that she needed a cat or dog so that she didn't have to live completely alone, as though being alone at night was some great tragedy. Fred had been the first man in her bed in over a year and a half, the first man she had had sex with in over a year. With two interviews for jobs like most people had, Lisa thought that she should try a dinner date and sex. Fred was available. Lisa bounced her head off her knees. She would rather have danced in front of him than have fucked him. She would rather have danced in front of any man.

Lisa let the air from the swamp cooler blow her hair back and cool her off. For the dancers' benefit, the **Stampede Club** had installed a cooler in a wall next to the dancing platform. As *Aquarius* started, Lisa pulled her arms out of the sleeves of her blouse and turned to face the men. They clapped and whistled, and Lisa started her dance. Lisa kept her body in angles rather than in curves and jerked when she moved. She wanted her dance to look primitive and unnatural. Sexy, she thought, but scary. She probably conjured up visions of sex with a space alien in the minds of the men who sat around the foot-high stage. She had rented the movie version of *Hair* and studied, as best she could, the film's editing, Twyla Tharp's choreography. She had stolen from Twyla as Twyla had stolen from Fosse to come up with a dance that was hers. And now, she revealed it in the second dance of her first set at the Stampede Club.

The long-haired, greasy-looking men in leather jackets and motorcycle boots, like the men back at Captain Hook's, not yet drunk or horny, stared quietly up at her trying to figure out what they were supposed to think of this dance. They had just watched the 250-pound bar maid with the hairy hump between her shoulders like a bull's, step onto the stage, which groaned from her weight, casually pull her halter top to her waist to expose enormous tits, then light two thin torches and swallow fire. They were confused.

Later in the night, Lisa would premiere another of her dances. She had watched *Flashdance*, and though she knew the routine was exhausting, she was determined to show her interpretation, complete with a chair and a bucket of water. At the Stampede, when she wasn't dancing, she had to sit with the men and coax them into buying her drinks that were always diet Cokes or tea, no matter what she ordered. But the Stampede let her do what she wanted to on stage. In return, she gave the Stampede and its clientele a little of what they wanted. She was their star attraction two nights a week. Her name was on the rented marquee outside by the frontage road next to IH-40.

This dance was all in her knees. Lisa let them go limp and dangled her arms in front of her, looking purposefully like an ape; then she let the resilience in her knees spring her back up.

Doris Rhodes got her the job with the Oklahoma Commission on the Arts, so she got to tell Gerry Obermeyer that she wasn't going to teach any P.E. classes to teenagers and old ladies. With a job that real people did, Lisa could afford to work at the Stampede part-time.

Lisa twirled, then stopped with her bent knees and spread them apart on either side of her. Her hands rested on her nearly horizontal thighs. She slowly straightened them inward to pull her breasts up against her chest. She licked a nipple. The music stopped.

The men didn't applaud. They looked at one another and at her. Then a husky man in a denim vest with no shirt underneath stood. A tattoo, an angry-looking, cigar-smoking Woody Woodpecker, was on his hairless chest. He started clapping. Other men started clapping and whistling. Several men rolled up dollar bills and held them out for Lisa. "Keep your goddamn money," the man in the vest said. "It ain't what she wants." He pulled off his black baseball cap with Harley written across the crown, stepped to the stage, extended his hand, and helped Lisa off the stage. Lisa wrapped both her arms around him and kissed him square on the lips, even sucked up some of his stale beer breath.

Lisa let go of the man and ran to the cramped women's restroom. A teenager leaned against the wall and smoked a cigarette. The cigarette was not helping the girl's nerves at all. She shook all over. Lisa methodically breathed in and out, then raised one leg, then the other to the sink and stretched. "You'll do fine," she told the youngster, who had a tattoo of a flower on the back of one shoulder and a tattoo of a bee on the front of her other shoulder. Tonight was her stripping debut.

The young stripper puffed on her cigarette, then exhaled. "I'll never be able to do that. It was beautiful." The new girl threw her cigarette on the floor, stomped on it, pulled her shoulders back, and wiped at her eyes. "My break's over."

"Don't worry," Lisa said.

The youngster looked at Lisa. Her face was young, innocent, ignorant, though she probably knew more and had certainly seen more than the students at Midwest City Community College. "Why do you go on? You're not a titty dancer. Why do you keep doing this?"

Lisa had come to know the answer; she thought how to explain it to the teenager. "I cannot not do it," she told the young stripper and felt for a moment like a teacher at Midwest City Community College. ■

BIT by the METAL

Oil Field Term for a Wound Suffered on the Rig

Bo Fralix had just closed the door on his wife and the woman who shared the semi-private room, Mrs. Griswald, and was sitting on a hospital couch when he first saw Joan Phelan. Bo was in the business of sizing people up quickly, but he saw nothing special about her at first, except maybe her enormous bag. She had that weary, numb look that civilians in a hospital get. Nurses always have fake smiles, and the doctors always have serious, crinkled looks, especially when, after a round of golf with Bo, they write out the hefty checks to the University of Texas.

Joan walked clumsily down the hall toward Bo, her purse tucked under one arm and her large bag with leather handles hanging down from the crook in her left arm and bouncing against her muscled calf. When she got near Bo, she swung around to look back at the door she had just closed, and Bo found something special about her, the way her denim skirt spread across her butt, the rear of a twenty-five-year-old woman. But when she turned back toward Bo and the stark hospital light caught the high points and darkened the sags of her face, Bo saw a woman fighting a relentless oncoming forty.

She dropped the large bag on the ground. It crumpled, and she dug into her leather purse, the small tasteful kind that screamed money and big donations at the alumni dinners and after-game parties that Bo organized. She pulled out a cigarette and hung it in her mouth. She dug into her purse again. "You have a light?" she asked Bo.

"I don't smoke, sorry," he said.

"Just as well." She crumpled the cigarette in her hand and let the strands of tobacco sift between her fingers into the ashtray beside the couch. She dusted her hands together, smiled again, and said, "I'm going to quit."

"Good idea," Bo said. "But," he added, nodding his head toward her relative's room, "is now a good time to try?"

"Withdrawal kind of counteracts the anxiety." She ran a hand over top of her head. "It's my mother. Who are you here to see?"

"My wife."

"I'm sorry," Joan said, not really sorry, as Bo could tell from the tone of her voice, but just social and polite, and by meeting her gaze, each daring the other to look away, Bo guessed that, this being Austin, she was a lawyer. Bo dropped his eyes, stood, and held out his hand, and said, "Bo Fralix."

Joan shook his hand, then dug into her purse to pull out one of her cards. Bo rolled it around in his fingers before he read it. "So you're a lawyer?"

Squinting and cocking her head to figure out how he guessed, Joan said, "More of a lobbyist. And soon, I hope to be a fund raiser for the local Democratic Party." She reached for her lips as though she had a cigarette, and when her fingers found no cigarette, she frowned and shook her hand. "And what do you do, Mr. Fralix?"

Bo stuck his hand into his sport coat, pulled out the

pocketbook, and handed her one of the cards with the embossed longhorn and UT. In black lettering next to his name was Alumni Director. "Maybe we have some common interests, Mr. Fralix."

"Probably so," Bo said.

They sat down together, and when they ran out of names, she said, "I hope your wife improves," leaned over, and pulled a stack of memos and forms out of her bag. Bo leaned the back of his head against the wall, and because the temptation outweighed the rudeness, closed his eyes. Lost for a moment in his worry, close to, but still too uncomfortable for sleep, Bo heard, "Oh, God, doesn't that hurt your head?"

Bo smiled without opening his eyes. "Kind of gets to your neck."

"Wait a second." Bo heard her dig in her large bag, then felt her breath on his forehead, and then the rough material of a sofa pillow slide between the crown of this head and the wall. "I bring it with me to take cat naps. One night I even curled up on this detestable bench."

"So you wouldn't dare call this a couch or a sofa, either."

"No. I wouldn't. Go to sleep if you like."

"No. I just want to close my eyes."

"Don't be silly. Go to sleep if you like."

"I'll snore."

"I've heard snoring, and I'm not planning to sleep. Good night." But Bo never got fully to sleep because he would roll his head to one side and open his eyes for a glimpse at the self-sufficient, cocky woman beside him thumbing through her work.

There were all sorts of women other than Joan willing to comfort Bo while his wife was in the hospital. At work, the director of recreational programs for continuing education would drop by and ask if she could do anything for him and Barbara. There were the consoling women clerks, the ones who found a pleasant bureaucratic niche within the gigantic UT system, prize jobs among the students and populace of Austin, who wanted to stay in Austin no matter what the job, the kind of woman Bo thought he'd marry rather than Barbara. When he got home to the house that he married into, ladies from Bo's and Barbara's prosperous neighborhood would bring over Tupperware filled with casseroles. Because he liked eating out better than the recipes of widows, newly divorced middle-aged ladies, or the idle wives of rich husbands, Bo's refrigerator was filling with Tupperware filled with mold.

Besides, as Barbara got worse, Bo spent his dinner hours with her at Brackenridge hospital. He would leave the guarded UT campus and drive or walk the ten blocks to the hospital. Then, after a hospital dinner and a talk with Barbara and Mrs. Griswald, Bo would drive home to his guarded, hilly, prestigious suburb in southwest Austin on the edge of the escarpment. He'd walk into his dark, ranch-style house and make his way through it by feel until he got to his study, where he'd turn on the light.

Because of the work that he brought home, because of the books that he wanted to read once he retired, Barbara had built Bo a study as a birthday present. Unaccustomed to the ways of the truly rich, Bo couldn't see why the rambling old house with rooms he had hardly ever seen needed another room. Barbara explained that it was more of a retirement present than a birthday present and that he would appreciate it once he had more time to enjoy it. Now, the study was his favorite room. Barbara had also bought Bo a BMW with the vanity license plates: ***Hook 'em Horns.***

Sometimes at night, when he got home, Bo liked to sit in his backyard in his shorts and clink the ice cubes in his bourbon against the sides of the glass and feel the breeze blow over his naked chest and legs. He'd look at the cornfield and the cedar trees beyond his unfenced backyard for the silhouette and sparkling eyes of the feasting, nervous, suburban deer, and he would remember hunting with his grandfather. Other nights, he'd go into his study and try to muster the concentration to read through the books that he wanted to read when he retired: Nietzsche, Marx, Freud. But usually, as he sipped his bourbon or squinted his eyes to understand the difficult philosophical questions in his book, Bo thought about his grandfather.

During the years when Bo's father started spending more time on the back roads peddling his insurance and his mother started spending more time at the Baptist Church, young Bo hung out at his grandfather's lawn mower repair shop and eventually became his grandfather's helper. John C. Plunkett, who had learned a little about blacksmithing, could oil and unclog the gears of a push mower and could study the parts of a gasoline motor long enough to fake fixing it. Mostly, he liked sharpening the blades. To John C., a sharp blade was a virtue, but he also liked the perverse thrill of tempting the blade to bite him. Not until he took a Texas history course and pieced together all the tales that John Calhoun Plunkett told him did Bo realize that the old man teaching him about the virtue and thrill of a sharp blade was closer to a cowboy than any of the stylized heroes he'd seen at the Lampasas movie theater. John C. had herded cattle, gotten stabbed in a whorehouse fight in Dallas, and done minor jail time all before he fathered Bo's mother. After the baby was born and he married her mother, John C. went off to the West Texas oil fields in order to earn enough money to support his wife and baby daughter and got bit by the metal when a chain flung loose from a pipe, coiled like a delirious snake, and nearly split John C. in two.

Besides the sharp edges, Old Man Plunkett liked women, and he taught Bo about what women liked; of course, the old man's notions were based on the comments of the old ladies he ran with. On Bo's first deer hunting trip with John C., before he was even allowed to carry a gun, just allowed to sit in the blind with the old man, John C. showed him a coordination trick with his hunting knife. For the next two mornings, rather than going out with him and sitting in the cold, looking for a deer, Bo stayed in the warm cabin and practiced putting his left index finger on the edge of the table, then whacking at it with a sharp butcher knife, then jerking his finger away just before the knife hit the table. He did this three times without slowing up, then four, until he could do it as fast as grandfather and as many times. "The ladies like that," John C. told his grandson.

When Bo showed his mother what her father had taught him, she told him not to do that trick anymore. His father just grunted and said, "Don't listen to that crazy old man," causing his mother to catch her breath and stare at her husband behind his back. Later, before he married Barbara, when he went out with friends, a date, or potential contributors, to impress them and honor his grandfather, Bo would pick up a steak knife and chop at his left forefinger.

When some scraggly hairs grew out of Bo's chin, his grandfather told him that women liked a smooth chin, so he lent Bo his straight razor for his first shave. Bo tempted the metal and went home with blood soaking through the bandage that John C. had put on his grandson's chin. As she pulled off the bandage, Bo's mother said that a young man like Bo shouldn't spend all his time with some obnoxious old man, that maybe Bo ought to consider going with her to the church and visit her *minister*, a nice Christian man. But Bo went back to see his grandfather and shaved off most of one eyebrow and put a deep cut on the bridge of his nose when his grandfather told him that women didn't like men with eyebrows that grew across their noses.

Bo's first job as his grandfather's helper was to drive the crumbling old Ford around Lampasas to pick up and deliver the lawn mowers. If the lawn mower owner was pretty or good natured, John C. would sharpen her blades for free, and if she was really special, he'd send his grandson over to mow her yard. With the money he made, Bo could make time with girls his own age.

Besides ladies and sharp blades, another of his passions that John C. let Bo in on was listening to football games on the radio. When Bo was a child, the old man would pick the boy up from his parents on a fall Saturday and sit in an iron lawn chair behind his shop with the boy on his lap, smoke a cigar, and listen to the Southwest Conference college games. The University of Texas was John C.'s favorite, and he explained the game to young Bo. John C. saved his money to buy the first TV in Lampasas just so he could watch the football games with his grandson.

Barbara had the bed nearest the door with her flowers from her neighborhood friends and daughters on the night stand beside her; Mrs. Griswald lay in the bed on the opposite side of the room, next to the window, with sports magazines and paper Dixie cups on her night stand. In the daylight, the two women kept the Venetian blinds open so that the beams of sunlight hit Mrs. Griswald's bed and stretched to the edge of Barbara's bed. Bo hated the room's intense whiteness and the feeling of the walls and ceiling and floor slowly moving in and up and down on him, and wondered how Barbara, after living most of her adult life in her large, landscaped house on the edge of the country, tolerated the room she shared with Mrs. Griswald. At first he wondered why, with all her money and insurance, Barbara wanted to share a room, especially with just anybody the doctors wheeled in.

For a while Barbara wanted, along with wigs, to read some of Bo's books. She trusted Bo's judgment about what she ought to read, so Bo brought her mostly long books, first *Great Expectations* and *Madame Bovary.* Then he brought books that he hadn't even read, *War and Peace* and *Anna Karenina.* The day he brought her *Anna Karenina* and a red wig, Barbara, a scarf around her head, took the styrofoam head with the wig on it, turned it around in front of her, picked up her half-frame glasses from her night stand, put them on, and squinted at the wig. "Mrs. Griswald," she said, "what do you think?" She held the wig so Mrs. Griswald could see it.

Bo heard Mrs. Griswald moan as she rolled over, then pushed herself into a sitting position to look at the wig. Bo looked at Barbara for some kind of order or explanation. Barbara gently shook her head, so he smiled to look at Mrs. Griswald. She had her wig on, something cheap and silver with one corner by her ear curled up. Her pink gown was crumpled and had greenish stains on it. A burp sounded from deep inside her, got up her throat, and almost out of her mouth. She swallowed hard. "Pretty, lovely," she said.

"Good job, Bo," Barbara said.

"And you said he doesn't know anything about wigs," Mrs. Griswald said.

Barbara waved her hand at Mrs. Griswald as if she were slapping her and said, "Shush, don't let on to Bo that we talk about him."

"Yeah, no telling what else she knows about me," Bo said and darted his eyes between his wife and Mrs. Griswald. Mrs. Griswald watched him, raised one eyebrow, and tried to giggle, but another burp caught in her throat.

Bo quickly shifted his head toward Barbara. And when she cocked her head to look through the bottom of her glasses and said, "Dear, are you all right?" Bo quickly moved to the side of Mrs. Griswald's bed.

"Should I get a nurse?" Bo asked.

"Lord, no. You get a little gas on the stomach, and excuse me, Bo, but you belch," Mrs. Griswald said.

Barbara and Mrs. Griswald laughed, but Bo didn't. And Barbara, when Bo looked at her, gently shook her head.

"Bo, help me up and to the bathroom, I want to try on the wig," smiled Barbara. "I feel so old when I use that thing." She pointed to the aluminum walker that the hospital had given her.

"I am old, and I don't like it," Mrs. Griswald said.

Barbara threw her legs over the side of the bed and as Bo helped her up, she put an arm around him and kissed him on the cheek. Bo caught a whiff of her sour breath, the result of medicine breeching mouthwash. His wife leaned into him, Bo put his arm around her, and he felt his wife's ribs along her sides where once she had a roll of middle-aged fat that she fought with a Stairmaster and a bicycle.

When Bo got Barbara into the bathroom and shut the door behind her, Mrs. Griswald patted the edge of her bed and said, "I'm not contagious." Bo sat down on her bed and could smell the same stink on Mrs. Griswald. It was as if the chemicals in Barbara's and Mrs. Griswald's bodies were seeping out of their pores. "She misses her house," Mrs. Griswald said. "You ought to bring over some of her stuff."

Bo giggled and said, "I'd have hoped she missed me."

Before Mrs. Griswald could say anything, Barbara came out of the bathroom as a redhead. She stepped out and spread her arms like an actress taking applause, and Mrs. Griswald did applaud, her hands straight up, her fingertips and palms coming together perfectly with quick blows, hands hardly spreading, the way a child claps. Bo, when he heard Mrs. Griswald's applause and looked at her, clapped his hands. Barbara laughed and stepped farther out toward the middle of the floor, turned a circle, laughed some more. "Honey," Bo said, "be careful." Mrs. Griswald laughed and kept clapping, belching once.

"I always wondered what I would look like with red hair," Barbara said.

Mrs. Griswald poked Bo with her elbow. "Before it turned gray, my hair was red."

Bo wandered around in the dark house that was Barbara's and her ex's, not really his, and listened to his ice cubes clink against the sides of his glass. A shiver started in the small of his back and went up his spine to his shoulders, shaking him the whole way because he had on only his underwear. Being charming was what he was good at. It was why he was director of alumni affairs, wining and dining in tuxedo or jeans. It was what he had learned from his grandfather, what he had refined in school, what had allowed him to marry a woman from elevated social circles.

When he saw her at a fund raiser, Bo recognized Barbara as a member of that group whose freedom from want kept them young and taught them easy courtesy, manner, and graciousness. Rather than stopping that hunt for women with one of the pleasant, beautiful, younger clerks or coeds whom he met, Bo married into a protected life with Barbara. He spent just one year in the large house with Barbara's youngest daughter; then the daughter went off to college, and Bo got a BMW and a study.

As Bo made it back to Freud, spine-down on his leather easy chair, he remembered reading that certain hereditary traits skipped a generation.

Before Bo was even born, the churches in Lampasas put away their squabbles about the true nature of Christ in order to create a social club for retired people and a recreation center for young people, but they wouldn't serve beer. Once he met a lady at a social club, John C. would invite her to accompany him to one of the two bars in Lampasas that specialized in serving beer to the old men. Besides the social club, Bo's grandfather liked to take his "lady friends" to dances held on Saturday nights in different small towns around Lampasas and to the nice bar in the Lakeview Hotel, although there was no lake to view in Lampasas. A couple of times, Bo double-dated with John C.

When teenage Bo complained about his colorless, boring father, whose rural insurance business didn't seem nearly as exciting as sharpening ladies' lawn mower blades, John C. explained, "It isn't what a man does, but what he is. It isn't your father's job, but his own nature that makes him such a tight ass." John C. hesitated while Bo nodded. "Which is why your mother spends so much time at church. You understand, Bo?" Bo nodded again, but of course, he didn't understand in the way his grandfather was wanting him to. "I was a pretty lousy father myself, but I was hoping for more for your mother. All that was around here for your mother was ignorant ol' cedar-choppin' country boys. So when your daddy showed up in town smellin' of lilac water, Yankee manners, business wizardry, your mother thought he was the best she'd ever do. He'd been married once, got kids somewhere. You understand, Bo?" Bo nodded again.

When her affair with her *minister* became public

knowledge, Bo's mother's minister quit the church and went off to Fort Worth to find other work. Bo's mother went with him. And Bo's father moved his business farther west to Brownwood. Both of Bo's parents asked him to go with them. But because he had two years yet to go in high school and was nearly grown anyway, they decided to let him stay where he wanted, with his grandfather.

On a long night after visiting hours, dreading the walk through Barbara's dark house, Bo sat on the couch with Joan's ugly, rough-textured pillow under his arm. When she came out of the room that held her mother and let the door swoosh shut behind her, Bo smiled and waved the pillow. Dressed in a faded pair of jeans and tennis shoes, her natural-looking, dirty blonde hair pulled into a bun, one strand loose and dangling to the side of her face, no makeup, looking tired, her large bag bouncing against her calf, she swayed a little, then lifted her feet more sprightly as she walked toward Bo. Joan frowned and cocked her head when she reached Bo. "Keep it," she said.

"You wouldn't want to give this up."

She dropped a shoulder to reach into her large bag and pulled out an identical pillow. "I got three for five dollars at a Kmart."

"I'll treasure this." Bo slipped it behind his head and leaned against it.

After a smile, Joan walked down the hall, and Bo watched her go, her jeans tight across her rear end, her bag bouncing against her calf. She stopped and said, "By the way, you didn't snore last week."

"That's a relief."

Bo had not taken his eyes off her, and she returned his gaze. "Let's have a Coke, a cup of coffee. Somewhere off this floor, outside this hospital."

"Where?"

"Anywhere, just out."

They walked to the back entrance of the hospital and saw through the rain **J's** 24-hour Cafe across the street. "Rain," Joan said.

Bo smiled. His office, the hospital, his study, months going by, seasons, the city changing. "Rain?"

"Do you have an umbrella?"

"No." Bo sniffed to smell the late winter shower, and time and season made sense to him again. A sloppy, damp February. He stuck his hand into the rain, shook from the chill it gave him. Joan sneezed.

Joan grunted as she hoisted the large bag over her head. Bo grabbed the end closest to him and pulled himself up under the bag and smelled the freshness of Joan's breath when she smiled at him. With the large bag over their heads, Bo bending slightly because he was taller, they ran on tiptoes through the puddles in the street, splashing water into their shoes. Midway across the street, Joan dropped her end, and Bo caught the bag in his outstretched arms and cradled it for a moment. She laughed. Then they ran separately across the street and under the awning of **J's**. When Bo handed her the bag, she shook it, then ran her hands down her thighs, pasting her wet jeans to her legs. "We're soaked," she said and started for the door, but Bo stayed where he was, watching the rain.

"You coming in?"

"I want to watch the rain."

"We can watch it from a window."

"I'd rather watch it from here."

"I'm going to go in and get warm."

"Be there in a minute."

Bo watched the splashes and the reflections in the wet street, exhaled, getting rid of the hospital smell, and breathed deeply, pulling the fresh smell of the rain into his lungs. He thought about the hot, humid day and the fresh, rainy night his grandfather died, then went into **J's** to meet Joan.

J's 24-hour Cafe was one of those dingy, all-night places on the verge of going broke. A cook was behind the grill clanging pots and pans, and a waitress sat at the counter on a swivel stool turned toward the front window, watching the rain. Joan sat in a booth next to the window. Bo sat down across from her, and the waitress came up with two menus.

"Coffee," Joan said.

"Two," said Bo.

The loose strand of Joan's hair dripped a bead of rainwater on the table. Her smile made deep lines in the corners of her eyes. Her blue eyes almost convinced Bo to call her a girl rather than a lady. The waitress came back with the coffees and set the coffee cups in front of them. Joan reached for the Sweet 'n Low in the rack on the table, and Bo sipped his coffee.

"Have you done this before?" Joan asked, and she slapped the packet of Sweet 'n Low against the heel of her upturned palm.

"Had coffee?"

"No, watched someone, someone, geez, never mind." She opened the Sweet 'n Low and shook the packet over her coffee.

"Have you?"

She looked up. Her smile dropped, then came back. "No."

"My grandfather first. Then my father."

Joan sipped her coffee, wrinkled her nose, added more Sweet 'n Low. "Nothing tastes right anymore."

"No one to help out?"

"My brother lives in Oklahoma City." She tried the coffee again, then asked, "Do you have any family to help?"

Joan reached into her bag and pulled out a pack of cigarettes and stuck one in her mouth. "Have a light?"

Bo chuckled. "I thought you quit."

"Makes me eat too much sugar."

Bo reached across the table and pulled the cigarette out from between her lips and crumpled it up. "Well, you're a charming guy," she said.

"I'm paid to be charming. Hell, I've teed-off with Darrell Royal, Willie Nelson, Earl Campbell."

"What about *kind*?" she said, and dug into her large bag and pulled out a pack of Kleenex, then blew her nose. Bo slowly reached across the table, lightly placed his forefinger on the top of her palm. Joan stared at his hand for a moment, then up at him. "What's your real name, Bo? Shouldn't the director of alumni affairs introduce himself by his real name?"

"I can forgive my father of most of his nature except for the name that he gave me. Bo looks good on the back of a belt and is cheap to engrave into the leather, which I liked well enough as a kid, when I was basically destined to be a cedar-cutting redneck. But I have no James or Howard to fall back on. My legal name, the name my father gave me, is Bo."

Joan placed her hand on the top of Bo's hand. "Did you ever see Bailey Waller play football?"

"Third Wishbone Quarterback. Darrell used to like those small, wiry, white Texas country boys."

"Bailey, my ex-husband, was from Houston."

"I played golf with Bailey, too."

"Bailey couldn't play golf."

"You're telling me."

The wind rattled the windowpane next to him, and Bo looked out of the window at the drops of rain streaking down the glass. Joan squeezed his hand, and because Barbara was far out of his mind and his grandfather seemed close by, Bo scooted across his side of the booth, sat next to Joan, and put his arm around her shoulders. He was, after all, a charming guy, and he could smell the same perfume that was on her pillow the week before.

Bo never met a visitor of Mrs. Griswald's. She mentioned friends or people she heard about or read about, but never a relative. Barbara once told him that the minister of Park Hills Presbyterian Church came by to see Mrs. Griswald. She didn't talk much to him, and his visit was short, perfunctory, and he left her a prayer book she never read.

On one particular visit, Bo walked in, saw Barbara, her red wig on, in Mrs. Griswald's bed. "Honey," Bo said in the direction of the bed, wondering why they had switched beds. Barbara, in her bed with a sheet pulled up to her nose, snorted in the way she did when she forgot herself. Mrs. Griswald, in the red wig, clapped, her fingers straight up, fitting perfectly together, like a child. She giggled.

Barbara had on Mrs. Griswald's silver wig with the corners turned up and looked, to Bo, the age she should have been to be dying of cancer. On the other hand, to Bo, Mrs. Griswald wasn't helped by the red wig. "We traded wigs," Barbara said.

"For keeps?"

"Sure."

"Barb, that was a $400 wig."

"Bo!" she said, banged her fist on her bed, glared at Bo.

Bo looked up at Mrs. Griswald. "Who's to see us anyway?" Mrs. Griswald laughed, and Barbara glared at Bo.

Another time, Barbara called during the week and told Bo to order Mrs. Griswald some flowers from the hospital flower shop because it was Mrs. Griswald's and Barbara's four-month anniversary.

When Barbara once left the room for radiation, Bo stayed in the room to play spades with Mrs. Griswald. Mrs. Griswald held her cards up in arthritic fingers that looked like they used to be delicate, stared long and deliberately at her cards, giggled before she took a trump, frowned after Bo took one. The betting was her idea, and she giggled when Bo let her win $2.76 from him.

While they were playing, Bo asked her about herself. "Nothing much," she said. "A little old lady who once wasn't a little ol' lady."

"How old is your wife?" she asked Bo.

"Too young," Bo said.

Mrs. Griswald looked up from her cards. "I'm glad to have her. I was in here by myself for nearly a month. Gets lonesome. Course being in the hospital is lonesome even with a roomie." She slapped a card on top of Bo's for a trump and giggled.

"I want to thank you," Bo said, and then his tongue got caught in his mouth when Mrs. Griswald looked up at him.

"For beating your ass?" Mrs. Griswald asked and giggled.

"For helping me watch Barbara."

"I'm not watching her," Mrs. Griswald said.

"You're helping me *watch*," Bo said, then continued before Mrs. Griswald looked back down at the cards. "I don't really know her that well. We haven't been married that long, not really, not like the usual people who come in here. Her daughters know her better. Her ex-husband was married to her longer. But it's just kind of fallen on me to be the one to watch. And maybe it helps if you have someone to . . . ." And Bo, the charmer, the man with just the right word, tried to twist his tongue around the right word, "to *witness*."

"Like I said," Mrs. Griswald said, "none of us got much choice. Barbara's a good witness, too. What else can she do?" And before Bo could say more, Mrs. Griswald found more evidence of their point. "Here, look," she said. She clenched her teeth and lifted her lips like a horse does. Her teeth were almost brown.

"That's what gave me cancer. I used to smoke unfiltered Luckies when I was a young woman. Only at home, though. People at that time thought ladies shouldn't smoke. Eventually, I said what the hell and smoked in public. Then, wouldn't you know, doctors find out smoking kills you." She shook her head, then looked back at her cards. "You can't tell."

"No justice," Bo said.

She cocked her head to one side and held her hand over the bed where the cards lay. She looked up from her cards. "No. No. There is some justice. Some kind of . . . of ironic justice. It makes sense – eventually. Don't you think?" Then she chuckled and continued with the game.

"I can see the irony," Bo said, thinking first about Barbara, then about his grandfather, then about Joan, "but not the justice."

While Bo was working with him, John C. once lifted up his shirt and nodded his chin toward the long, red scar that made a slanting coil around his abdomen. "That's where the metal bit me. I teased it but wasn't fast enough," he said. "Feel it." And Bo traced the rough, hard, lumpy scar. "You stay away from rough necking," John C. said. "I don't want to see you get one like that. But you got to decide what you gonna do with yourself. You wait too long, you end up some old man sharpening old ladies' lawn mower blades."

After Barbara came to from her first operation, the nurses let Bo stay in the room while they changed the dressing. Barbara looked at him as though she wanted him to see what the doctor had done: given her a long, fresh scar that seemed to have mangled her breast then curled up under her armpit. Later, since he had gotten used to the first scar, he was able to change dressings for the wound where the metal bit her the second time.

When Bo graduated from high school and watched his friends go off to college or join the service, go anywhere or do anything to get away from the boredom of sipping sodas at the Dairy Queen, going to a beer joint, conning a beer from a waitress who knew you were too young, trying to get your fingers into the lacy panties of a cheerleader at the drive-in movie theater, well, Bo decided to stay with what he knew, the lawn mower repair business.

After a couple of years, the draft called Bo away for a stint in Germany to defend freedom from Communists, but as soon as he was discharged, he came back to Lampasas, rented his own room, and hung around his grandfather's business. John C. drove the boy to Austin and made the lanky kid walk across the UT campus with him. Bo remembered clunking along the campus sidewalk in his thick-soled boots looking at fraternity boys in penny-loafers and sweaters, even though it was too warm on a central Texas autumn day to be wearing a sweater.

They walked across the drag for a beer and sat outside **Scholz'** beer garden, and John C. said, "A young stud like you ought to be out chasing split tails instead of working with some limp-dick old man."

"Well, how about you give me the truck, and I chase a few split tails while I'm here," Bo said.

John C.'s laugh got caught in his throat, and he coughed, then chased the cough with a big drink from his beer. "How about you and me go look at the football stadium."

On the ride home, boozy but not yet drunk, Bo listened to his grandfather remembering. "I wished I'd chased more tail when I was a young man," he said, as his head bobbed, and the lights from the speedometer lit his drooping jowls. He pulled his eyes from the blacktop to look at Bo. "I ran a few women there even while I was married to your grandmother."

Bo peered into the dark and listened to his grandfather's bullshit. Sounded like a romantic Mexican song.

"Alice was plump. The little folds in her behind shook when she got naked. A waitress in Midland. I figured she had done a little whoring, so I left her to come back to my wife, your momma".

"John C," Bo said, "you think I ought to ever get married, or just stay single and chase tail?"

"I think you ought to go to college so you can chase a better class of tail," and John C. turned his face from the road to stare at his grandson. Bo noticed the red tint in his grandfather's eyes and took the remark as command.

Bo went to college and learned about charm, books, fraternities, The New Left, and the tastes of young women (they didn't mind about a young man with just one eyebrow as his grandfather's widows did). He liked it so well he went to graduate school and dodged bullets on his way to a graduate seminar when Charlie Whitman climbed the tower and started shooting at people. With a graduate degree, he walked a few blocks from campus, got a job writing decrees for the state legislature: "Be it thereby declared by this legislative body that John Doe shall henceforth be proclaimed as the father of Texas fruit and vegetable retailing." Then, with the help of a few friends from his fraternity and the legislature, Bo got a job at the alumni affairs office at UT, so John C.'s grandson became a part of the makers and shakers, the pretenders and the charmers, the hangers-on and the drop-outs that clung to Austin.

Joan, too, Bo learned, was a slacker, a hanger-on. She had told Bo about her student days in Austin, then leaving with a husband and a law degree, only to come back to a brighter future in politics. And he saw himself in her when his future started to become real, and he saw in her the best of Lampasas girls and UT coeds and his sick, rich wife.

The meetings with Joan blended together for Bo. They went shopping at a mall, bought funny cards for her mother, his wife, and then for each other. They watched the sun set on the town lake while they ate sandwiches in his BMW. After they watched the rented Humphrey Bogart movie in Bo's study, Bo on his leather recliner, Joan on the sofa, her large bag beside her, she got up, curled into his lap, kicked off one shoe then the other, and rested her head against his shoulder.

After a kiss, Bo pulled himself out from under Joan and turned off the lights, and in the dark, he pulled her by the hand as he felt his way through the dark house to the master bedroom that he shared with Barbara. As he slid her blouse over her head, Bo lost the feeling of Barbara staring but wondered what his grandfather would say.

When they were in bed and she rolled on top of him, he felt that great, bone-deep need that he shared with his grandfather, and the memory of his grandfather let him know that Joan or someone like her had to happen. And, when Joan was once again curled into a ball with her head resting on Bo's shoulder, all Bo could feel was grateful and glad that it was not someone like Joan, but specifically Joan. And for the first night in a long time, Bo went to sleep easily and woke late, to the smell of the coffee Joan had made.

The day after his night with Joan, Bo stepped into Barbara's room and saw the sunlight coming in from the open window catching the yellow and white of the new carnations and wilting mums on Barbara's night stand. A light breeze blew the Venetian blinds, and the pastel blue curtains spread out over the light from the window. "How did you get the window open?" Bo asked.

"Mrs. Griswald attacked it with a nail file," Barbara said. Barbara was in her new brunette wig that resembled her natural color. Mrs. Griswald rolled away from Bo and faced the wall. Bo bent close to Barbara and asked, "Is Mrs. Griswald mad at me?"

"She's fine," Barbara said, "But how are you doing?"

"Okay."

Barbara patted the bed, and Bo sat beside her, and saw smoke rise from Mrs. Griswald's bed.

"Honey, is she on fire?" Bo said and pointed at Mrs. Griswald.

"It's nothing. Oh, Bo, did you bring a Sunday paper? We've been reading a series about the careers of women tennis players."

"No, I'm sorry. I forgot." Bo could not remember Barbara ever before being interested in celebrities.

"Mrs. Griswald," Barbara said in a raised voice toward Mrs. Griswald's bed. "It's almost 11:00."

Mrs. Griswald rolled over, smiling at Bo. She had a cigarette in her mouth and an ashtray in her hand and expertly flicked the ashes of the cigarette into the ashtray. "Shhh," she said. Barbara laughed.

"Mrs. Griswald!" Bo scolded.

"I walked to the fifth floor lobby in that damned old walker." She winked, "And bought my last pack of cigarettes." Barbara turned on the TV with her remote control. "Pre-game," Mrs. Griswald said to Barbara.

"San Antonio Spurs," Barbara said.

"Since when do you watch basketball games?" Bo asked Barbara.

Mrs. Griswald asked, "You like basketball?"

"Only **UT**," Bo said.

Barbara smiled at Bo and rubbed his leg, "The paper." When Bo got back to the room with the *Austin American Statesman*, Mrs. Griswald had an unlit cigarette in her lips and was waving her hands and commenting about the game. Barbara giggled at her and sometimes asked her questions. She raised her nose to look through her half-frame glasses at the game. When Bo gave the paper to Barbara, she looked at the front page, pulled out the *Star* and the sports section and had Bo hand them to Mrs. Griswald.

Barbara looked through the paper very slowly and occasionally looked up at the game while Mrs. Griswald jerked her head continuously from the paper to the TV set. The breeze grew stronger and rippled the pale blue curtains and rattled the Venetian blinds. The sun grew brighter and the whiteness in the room had none of the intenseness of artificial hospital light, but a kind of softness. Bo sat in a chair next to Barbara's bed and pretended to watch the game while he rubbed Barbara's arm and touched her cheek with the back of his hand, as though he were trying to remember the feel of his wife.

Over the weeks, while Bo spent his nights with Joan, Barbara continued to chat about what she and Mrs. Griswald had done the previous week, about the ridiculous game shows and soap operas Mrs. Griswald watched, about how far she had gotten in *War and Peace*. Once, as he exited his wife's door, he saw Joan at her mother's door and nodded to say hello. She said, "Hi." They walked separately down the hall, she taking the elevator down after Bo. But in the parking lot, Bo waited next to her car, kissed her when she walked up, then drove to her apartment.

If she had known, with all her good breeding and grace, Barbara would probably have nodded her head, as she did when her girls were young and troubled, and said, "Now I can see that. But let's think about this."

As for the girls, they had declared an uneasy truce with Bo. They came when they could, called weekly, left messages. They didn't know how to act in their old rooms without their mom in *their* house, only this strange man whom Mom had decided to marry. But they were grateful, too, because their mom at least had this man around to comfort her in their absence. Even the ex-husband showed up, and Bo gave him a room in the large house, phoned Joan and asked her to give him a night off, and, with nervous deer watching, drank bourbon in the back yard with the old man who had paid for that back yard. And the ex-husband, who, with a new wife and family had all but forgotten about Barbara, thanked Bo for being with her.

One evening, after Bo stopped off for a few beers with old drinking buddies from UT – to forget, for a while, his nightly duties – and just at dusk, he walked into Barbara's dark room where a dim night-light lit the back of Barbara's red wig. Unless they were playing another trick on him, Mrs. Griswald had given the wig back. "Honey," Bo said, looking first at Barbara's bed, then toward Mrs. Griswald's bed. He stepped farther into the room, and the door shut behind him. "Honey. It's me." The red wig rolled toward him. Barbara was under it. "Barbara?"

"Shhh," she said and held her finger to her lips. She usually tried to put on makeup, but she had none on; so with her eyes red and swollen, with the wig bright under the light, she looked a dull gray with white and yellow splotches on her face. Bo reached down for her hand but barely brushed it with his fingertips as she rolled onto her back and looked up at the ceiling. "She was having trouble," Barbara said. "I called the nurses, and they took her out. Then they made her bed and drew the curtain." Barbara pushed herself up on one elbow and stared at Bo. "They will put somebody else in that bed tomorrow or the next day." She rolled her head away from him, and he barely heard her say, "I can't get used to somebody else. I don't have time." Bo sat beside her, and she pressed her head against his side, and he patted the side of her red wig. "Bo, please honey, get me a private room."

"Barbara, are you all right? Have they given you something? Do you want something?"

"I'm so sorry, Bo. Don't worry about me. There is nothing you can do for me. It is beyond us."

"What is?"

"Whatever it is that you are doing with your life outside of this hospital room. It is just okay, to be expected." Bo had to look at his wife's face to remind himself that it was not his grandfather talking. And when he saw her face, Barbara said, "Bo, please understand, honey. I'd like to be by myself tonight."

Bo got up and stood over Barbara. She smiled, and Bo left her to meet Joan. "You're not hurting anyone," Joan told him.

The fall before his grandfather died, Bo had driven up to Lampasas to watch Texas beat Arkansas and then Notre Dame in the Cotton Bowl for the national championship on John C.'s small black and white TV. After the Arkansas game, Bo gave John C. a football with *Best Wishes to our good friend, John C. Plunkett* written across its side and signed by the first ever wishbone-T backfield – James Street, Steve Wooster, Ted Koy, and Jim Bertelsen.

Late the next spring, John C. was left comatose by his stroke and didn't know that his daughter, her minister, and Bo had gathered in his Brackenridge hospital to watch him die. John C.'s breathing got caught in his throat, so a gurgling came out of his mouth. No matter how many times a nurse shut his mouth, the hinge of his jaw relaxed, the skin on his jowls stretched, and his mouth opened.

Bo's mother sat in a chair by the side of the bed and

cried for her father. Her minister, who had turned to selling insurance just like Bo's father, patted her on the shoulder. "Daddy always had a good heart," she said to her husband and Bo.

Spit formed on John C.'s lips; his exhaling blew the spit into a bubble that hovered above him for a minute; then the bubble burst. Bo said, "I've got to get out of here."

Bo's mother's minister stepped away from his wife and toward Bo, and said in the woeful tone of a mournful, wise Jesus, "Are you still too young to realize grief?"

"What do you know about him, me? You watch him," Bo said to the ex-minister but looked at his mother, "I'll remember him."

Bo's mother smiled. So Bo left his grandfather to slobber and gasp.

The day Bo's grandfather died was the day the whole country wore black arm bands to protest the war in Vietnam. In Austin, it was hot, humid, with the promise of a gully-cleansing rain that just wouldn't come. As the sun set, some of the people Bo saw as he walked down Eleventh Street from campus to the Brackenbridge hospital still wore their black arm bands.

The hippies who sold brocade pillows, T-shirts, bracelets, dope (if you asked the right ones), flowers, or just begged for money were pushing their carts or carrying their goods back to their shabby homes. Many of them were missing limbs because they were vets who got back from the war and dropped out of whatever there was to drop out of.

Bo got his hot, damp car and drove across the Colorado River to **Christie's** restaurant to meet the real reason he had walked out on his grandfather: a tall, braless girl with long hair held out of her face by a leather headband with a feather dangling from one side. Bo had made the date because he had been promoted to assistant director of alumni affairs, and in **Christie's** with his hippie date, as he shook the hands of jocks and contributors, he felt as though he had become a part of this city and wanted to hold on to that feeling of a future finally become real.

As they ate, a linebacker from the football team came to their table with his date, a blonde in a formal and gloves, and shook Bo's hand. A local doctor came up with his polite wife, who stood back from the table and stared at the hippie with Bo, and the doctor told Bo that he would make a contribution to Bo's newest scheme, UT salons, meetings of local professionals to discuss the events of the day.

After dinner, Bo's date insisted they drop by **Mother Earth's**; while members of a band called Navasota swung their long curly hair around and pounded out music that shook Bo in his tracks, Bo's date, in her blue-tinted glasses and bell bottoms, jumped up and down on the dance floor and swung her hair around.

Over the years, the girl stayed the same age and appeared many times in Bo's life. Sometimes she wore tight fitting Wrangler jeans and scooted her boots across the floor of the **Broken Spoke**; sometimes she wore an evening gown left over from a sorority party and went with Bo to the opera or symphony; once she had spiked hair and a diamond stud in one nostril and danced like she was on a pogo stick. As time went on, the girl began to major in things that didn't have a name but just some initials or an acronym nobody understood. Eventually, he married Barbara and then fell in love with Joan.

But that night, when his grandfather died, with this version of that girl, the over-worked air conditioning losing against the humidity, Bo made his way to the dance floor and tried to shout above the music to his date that she should get her own ride home. He left this girl and went back to Brackenridge hospital. As he got out of his car sweat-stained, whisker-stubbled, hot, the rain came down. The people crowded into restaurants or bars came out into the night, stared up at the sky, their clothes wet and pasted to their bodies, some taking off their clothes, and they stood, sloshed, or danced – braless, hairy, soaked, or even naked, in the rain. Over the years, this was the Austin that Bo liked best, but his grandfather was dying.

Chilled as he went into Brackenridge hospital's air conditioning, Bo walked into his grandfather's room and found only a candy striper folding the sheets. The sixteen-year-old cried when she told him that his grandfather had died.

Several years later, Bo heard about his father's death from his mother. Then his mother's minister died, and Bo began to pay the rent for the small apartment in Austin where his mother moved. Bo encouraged her to get out more and see some men.

When Bo told Joan he couldn't see her anymore, Barbara had gone from the private room Bo had gotten her to intensive care. When she heard Bo stumble through his rehearsed speech, Joan paced across his study and kicked at Freud lying spine down on the floor. "You self-deceiving son of a bitch," she said. "How long have you been thinking about this?"

"For years," Bo said, "before I ever married her."

Joan picked a pencil off the desk and pressed the point against her thigh and slid her fist down the pencil until it was touching her thigh. She reversed her fist, pressed the eraser against her thigh, and slid her fist down the length of the pencil once again. Then again.

Bo said, "She really is just this woman I married. If

not me, she has no one to be with her. I've had a good life, I've been lucky, you're part of my luck, but I've never given anything back. Never in my life have I done something noble."

"*Noble.* Funny fucking word from you. What about me?" Joan said. She raised the pencil and pressed the eraser against her forehead. "Oh, shit, you've got me being a cliché. Well, I won't be one. So Barbara gets *noble.* What do I get?"

"You got charm," Bo said, tried to laugh.

"You mean bullshit," Joan said. "You made yourself a part of my life." Joan caught her breath, "I don't think I can get through this without you. You've got some obligation here to me too, you know." She braced herself and said as though in court, "Who are you going to hurt?"

"It's got to be you," Bo said. "I can't figure any other way."

"Can I call you?"

"If you want."

"Oh, hell, I won't either," she said, threw the pencil down, grabbed her large bag, "I'll do it cold turkey."

Bo followed Joan through his house, turning on the lights so that she might find her way out, and as she stepped out the front door, the last words he got out were, "Maybe later, when . . . ." The door closed, and Bo wanted to know what his grandfather would say if he could know what Bo had just done. ■

POTENTIAL

From his office, Bailey Waller could see the late August sun cook Bob Compton's used car lot. He saw the heat rise off the asphalt, the glare from the new paint jobs and chrome trim. The asphalt was cracking, just like the mesquite-filled desert that threatened to overgrow I-20, which was just across the undeveloped commercial lot behind Compton's dealership. Bailey Waller sat in his glass-walled, air-conditioned office, where he should have felt protected.

He looked out at the lot and saw several figures in the heat and said *damn* to himself. Most people have the good sense not to look at cars at midday; they come before noon or after six o'clock. But a family of four wanted to buy a car, and Pooter Elam, Bailey's former teammate, college buddy, and home town Odessa boy, was showing them a five-year-old Buick. Pooter's hands worked like a TV preacher's as he steered the family against the fender of a Buick. Bailey got up from the seat. He watched Pooter pat at his sweating forehead with his fingertips, then hide his hands behind him and shake his fingers, flicking his sweat off. The belly Pooter had been growing since he and Bailey got out of college curled his belt down. Pooter had been a good tackle, Bailey thought.

Bailey slipped his hand into the pocket of his Jaymar slacks and pulled out the crumpled clipping from the employment section of Wednesday's *Odessa American*. He read it slowly. Peacock Military Academy needed an eighth grade football coach and history teacher. Bailey walked back to his desk, sat down behind it, and put the clipping in front of him, reading it over and over. Bailey, like most people his age, believed that certain things in your life turn it around for the better. Unlike most people, Bailey knew that he could have the important things if only he could see them coming. After all, he had potential. Every coach he had ever had said Bailey Waller had Po-tential, Po-tential, like it was two words. Mr. Bob Compton said he had it. Even his freshman history teacher said he had potential. It wasn't something he could define; he just knew potential was something that made getting what he wanted easy.

Bailey looked up, saw the shaking air-conditioner that poked through the cracked paneling, and the photographs that hung behind his desk. Mr. Compton had told him to put those particular pictures there. "Helps business," he said. The color photograph of Bailey in his football uniform, number 11. "Bailey Waller, quarterback," it said underneath.

"Everybody trusts a football player," Mr. Compton had said. Bailey didn't pose like some hot dogs, like he needed mustard, holding a football, sidestepping, giving a forearm, or growling like Pooter. No. He knelt and looked strong, forceful, competent. Full of potential. There was the newspaper clipping of Bailey and Bob Compton shaking hands. Mr. Compton was welcoming the All-American, who had ruined his knee trying out as a free-safety with the Houston Oilers, to the Compton Buick sales team. Next to it was Bailey again, strong, forceful, competent, and full of potential in his Salesman-of-the-Month photograph. And then there was a blank space on the wall. It matched the blank space on his desk. Only Bailey and Pooter knew what filled those blank spaces. Bailey hid the gold-framed photographs of Joan in his desk drawer. He spun around to his desk.

Bailey picked up the small, silver, aluminum model car with "Compton Buick" written across its side. He flipped the switch in the back of the car. The tiny headlights came on. Bailey turned the car around in his hands. Like most people his age, Bailey believed that he deserved better, but he had more faith than most people his age because he had potential. Beyond his deserving was a logical, reasonable expectation of getting better things. All he needed was to maintain his faith until he got his break. He had the clipping, and he had Bob Compton.

He got up from his desk, walked out into the hall, opened the door to the heat outside. He let the door go and walked down the steps. The hot aluminum handrail seared his palm. He walked between a '78 Chevy Malibu and an '81 Datsun and stopped to look at Pooter. The asphalt burned through his shoes. Pooter had stopped his movement, his hands down at his sides, his mouth forming a lazy O. Bailey remembered Pooter as a freshman tackle at the University of Texas, a big, dumb, homesick, West Texas boy. Bailey walked through the used car lot and into the glassed-in palace that displayed the new cars. He glanced over his shoulder at Pooter, who looked at him, then back toward his customers, like he was trying to decide between them and Bailey. Bailey could see that Pooter was still plagued by the same habit that hurt him in football, that habit of analyzing even his physical moves and getting paralyzed, instead of acting on instinct and desire.

He stepped into the showroom and turned to his right. The showroom was cool. It chilled the sweat that ran down his back and stained the collar of his fitted shirt. He looked at the four new Buicks, shiny with chrome and buffed paint, parked on the thick red carpet showroom. Though he had worked there for five years, Bailey still wondered how they kept the cars from leaving tracks in the carpet. He stopped to look at the assistant manager, Tulley Lee, with his telephone pressed to his ear. Tulley Lee was a fill-in announcer for the pro-wrestling on Saturday and Wednesday nights. Bailey knew that his future with the car company was to become someone like Tulley. "Compton in?" Bailey asked. Tulley jerked his thumb toward Bob Compton's office down the hall.

Bailey walked down the hall and looked at the paintings that Mr. Compton had bought second-hand from the Holiday Inn. He walked slowly to give himself every opportunity to do everything properly. The point of no return, he thought.

Mr. Compton had been good to him. After he spent a summer trying out for the Houston Oilers, after two years of living in Austin, bar tending and waiting for Joan to get her law degree, and after she got the degree and a job in Odessa as a corporate lawyer for Getty Oil, Mr. Compton hired him because of Pooter's recommendation.

Mr. Compton didn't make him dress up in chicken outfits and sell cars on Sunday morning TV commercials that cut into old movies and church services. "I run an honorable, dignified business. I'm not going to embarrass you," he told Bailey. He kept his word even when the automobile business got bad. Compton had inherited his daddy's prime real estate and became one of the city's biggest car dealers. More, he was a loyal UT alumnus, and though he had never been a jock, he took care of athletes, to repay them for their services, he always said. More important, Compton contributed to Peacock Military Academy, had a boy enrolled there. Teaching was a more honorable profession than selling cars, and Joan would be surprised and glad to see Bailey doing something important and honorable. Living up to his potential. He lifted his knuckles to the door to knock.

"Wait," Bailey heard behind him. He turned. Pooter was breathing heavily and sweating. He put his hand below his chin and caught some beads of sweat before they could stain his shirt or tie. "You gonna do it?"

"Yeah," Bailey said.

Pooter wiped his face with his hand. "What the hell for?"

Bailey didn't feel like explaining again, shrugged his shoulders. Pooter's face wrinkled, and Bailey knew he would have to give him some kind of an explanation. "Look at you, overweight, sweating like a pig."

"You think you ain't gonna sweat being a coach?"

"It ain't wasted sweat when you're a coach. Goes toward something important."

"You talking bullshit, son. You remember high school. You gonna make less money."

"Money's not important. You got to live up to what you are capable of doing."

"More bullshit." Bailey turned away from Pooter because he just couldn't make him understand. "Shit. You like a one-legged duck swimming in circles." Pooter said. "Hell, I gotta get back to my customer."

Bailey turned around, "You left a customer standing out in the sun?"

"Yeah," Pooter said. "You not gonna let me even try to argue you out of it?"

"No." Pooter hesitated, turned slowly, then raced down the hall back to his customer. Bailey turned back to the door and knocked.

He opened the door and looked across the large carpeted office with a built-in bar and expensive aluminum and leather office furniture. He looked at the mahogany desk, clear of all paper, only the opaque protective vinyl sheet on top of it. He looked at Mr. Compton behind his desk.

Bailey walked up to the desk, reached into his pocket, and pulled out the newspaper clipping. He stopped in front of the chair that sat in front of Mr. Compton's desk. "There's a coaching job in Midland," Bailey said, and gently placed the clipping on Mr. Compton's desk. Mr. Compton picked up both arms of his gold, half-framed glasses that hung by a chain around his neck, put them on, grabbed the clipping, read it. He looked up.

"Sit down," he told Bailey. Bailey sat in the leather chair that was in front of the desk. As Mr. Compton took his glasses off, Bailey saw the large diamond ring on his right forefinger sparkle, the garnet ring on his pinky shine. On Mr. Compton's left hand was a simple gold wedding band. "Tell me how you decided I can help you get this job." From the tone in Bob Compton's voice and the beginning of a smile on his face, Bailey knew things were starting well.

He was ready with his answer; he had practiced. "I thought when I didn't make pro that it was meant to be that I stick with football by coaching. But I didn't have the degree complete nor the teaching certificate." Mr. Compton leaned back in his chair. "Now, this job gives me a chance. Like you said, and what I appreciated so much when you hired me, was that you said you would always help out." Bailey hesitated to get it just right. "I know with all your interests . . . ." Compton held up his hand, palm out. Bailey knew it meant for him to stop, Bob Compton was always quick and to the point.

"This is not exactly some college coaching job where you become the next Darrell Royal."

Bailey was ready for that: "I know it isn't like I'm gonna be a real coach, just like playing flag football with Pooter and a bunch of oil rig trash ain't real football. But it's doing something important." Bailey looked at Mr. Compton, then scooted to the edge of his chair. "When you're in a West Texas town that don't have a semi-pro team, or even a Lone Star Conference college team, all that's big is schoolboy football. The only way for me to be important here is to coach high school football."

Compton chuckled and said, "This is not exactly Permian High School with a state championship trophy every year or so, either."

"It's a start," Bailey said. "You know I got potential. All I need is the start."

"Potential is one thing, Bailey," Compton said. "Getting by another."

"I do better than get by."

Mr. Compton wrinkled up his forehead, then smiled. "I can get you the job, Bailey, but I'm gonna miss you." He took a breath, then continued. "My son plays for Peacock. I really would like for him to play." Bob Compton smiled at Bailey, and Bailey knew he meant nothing dishonorable or questionable. Bailey nodded his head. "Why don't you go see these folks tomorrow?"

Bailey walked out of Mr. Compton's office knowing the thing had been done, the momentum started, and he knew his potential would carry him through. He told Pooter and took him to lunch at the **Steak And Ale** restaurant. After lunch, in the Steak And Ale parking lot, Bailey watched Pooter try to squeeze his stomach behind the steering wheel of his MG. Pooter showed up at college with that car. Yes, he had gotten bigger, but the car hadn't.

"Why don't you get a bigger car? They'd give you a demo."

"You get used to some things," Pooter said. Bailey asked him to take him by Joan's office. "That why you took me here, so you could embarrass yourself in front of her again?"

"Come on, it's right down Parkway, right down the street."

"You're nuts, son," Pooter said. "Get her out of your head."

"I'm just gonna tell her about my new job," Bailey said, thinking how glad she would be to hear.

"Big deal."

"Just drop me by and wait. I'll be right out."

"Just busting for her to piss you off again, ain't you?"

"All right, goddamn it. I'll phone her after work." But Pooter dropped him off at the building and waited in the parking lot.

Joan's maiden name was added to the end of the string of attorney's names. They had several suites, all decorated with finer furniture than Bob Compton had. Bailey had seen her office twice. Seeing it, and having gone with her for the interview in San Antonio, he couldn't believe that she had ever considered being a public defender in a shabby office in the San Antonio courthouse. He walked into her suite and asked her secretary to buzz her. She wasn't in. Bailey pulled out one of his cards, flipped it over, and wrote, *call me* on it. He decided against putting *love*, then signed it. He gave it to the secretary, then took the stairs down to the lobby of the building.

When he got back out into the lobby of her office building, Bailey saw the elevator doors close in front of Joan's face. He caught himself just before he yelled to her. He raced back up the stairs. As he went up the steps, he thought he must not look too eager when he caught her. He stopped Joan just as she was grabbing the doorknob to her suite. "Joan," he allowed himself to shout, and smiled as he ran to her. He could not tell for sure if she pretended not to hear; she opened the door and started to go in. He was just able to grab the door knob from her and slam the door shut. Joan gasped.

"Oh, Bailey! Jesus," she said.

She still said *Jesus* in her own way, Bailey thought, trying to cram both syllables into one, while everybody else in West Texas stretched the word out into three or four. He was breathing too heavily to talk. He paused to catch some air and look at her. With her hair pulled back behind her head, with just enough make-up on to let you know she wore make-up, she looked older, but much prettier. She used to look pretty, Bailey thought, back when Pooter called her an Earth Mother. Now she was lovely.

"Oh, Bailey, please stop the visits and the calls. Please."

"I got something to tell you."

"It's over between us."

"I didn't come here for that." Bailey breathed in deeply to deliver the news, "I'm gonna coach football and teach, do something important, like you said." He waited for a hug or a short friendly kiss. Joan's eyelids dropped, then lifted, and she smiled sweetly. She kissed the tips of her fingers, then gently pressed them against his forehead.

"Do you think you can do it?" she asked.

"Sure."

"Bailey, you're gonna just have to learn." She stopped, then turned to the door to go in. Bailey grabbed her elbow, squeezed it, and pulled her away from the door. She gasped at first, pulled her elbow toward her side and dipped her shoulder. "Bailey," she said sternly.

"What do you mean?" Bailey said.

"Nothing, let go." Bailey let go of her elbow. She opened the door and went in, closing it behind her, not even saying goodbye or congratulations.

She was the one who said that he ought to quit selling cars, first gave him the idea of doing something important. Bailey swung at the wall, hit it hard. Then again. He was sure anybody inside the suite heard him. He wanted to kick in the door of her suite and shout to all the associates, "I used to fuck her!"

Midland had all the oil executives, the millionaires. Mr. Bob Compton lived in Midland. Odessa had the good football teams. But a year at Peacock might move him on. When Bailey got to the Academy, Mr. Compton had already called. He got the job without any problem. He didn't need transcripts or degrees. He just had to leave them with the promise that he would go to school during the summers and get some kind of a degree. He called Mr. Bob Compton to thank him, and Mr. Compton told him to take the week off from selling cars to prepare for school.

When he got home, out of habit, he picked up the telephone to call Joan. He knew he shouldn't have, but he did call her, and he asked for his old play book. She briefly congratulated him on his job, then said she had no idea where his play book was. When the conversation reached a lull because Bailey was trying to decide whether or not to accuse her of not caring about his play book or lying about it to him, she politely said, "Good luck," and hung up. Bailey thought about going over to her house, his former house, and tearing it apart until he came across the play book, but he found it at the bottom of a cardboard box labelled *football stuff*.

During his week off, he woke late in the mornings, but after he woke, he ran and pumped weights to get into better shape for his job. He borrowed a college textbook for an American history course from a coed who lived above him. In the afternoon, he took the book and a six-pack of beer to the pool to study. He always bought bottled beer. Somehow the glass made the beer taste better. He liked to feel the beer in his throat and his belly as well as taste it. He concentrated on the feel and the taste of the beer as he drank it. And when he got bored with studying, he invented a game. He threw into the pool an inner tube that one of the renter's kids left poolside; then he would try to throw his bottles through the hole of the tube as he emptied them. Bailey liked to watch the ripples and the small waves the bottles caused gently lap up under the lip at the pool's edge.

One morning, because somewhere in his memory of high school, when long hair meant a lack of discipline, or maybe because he was thinking of his first meeting Joan, back when she was a hippie barber, he got a haircut.

Back then, he was a sophomore in college who made the headlines of the *Daily Texan* because of his performance at spring training. He was full of potential, and hippie Joan was a barber at a time before barbers became hair stylists. It was popular then for a football player to have hair just long enough to have a tuft stick out from under the back of his helmet. It looked good on TV. Now, getting a haircut from a middle-aged woman in Odessa, he thought about how much he had wanted Joan the first time he saw her in that shop in Austin, just off Guadalupe Street, with hippie vendors selling brocade pillows in front of it.

The floor of the barber shop was bare wood. The ripped and scarred leather-covered chairs, some spitting up their insides, still had razor strops hanging beside them. An overhead fan circulated the stale, uncooled air. A man with a shaved head and a gold earring cut a little boy's hair, and Joan cut the boy's brother's hair. Joan wasn't so much good-looking but looked good doing what she did, cutting hair. She looked like a dancer because she didn't wear shoes when she cut hair. Getting a haircut from her was like dancing with her. Only later did Bailey learn that she went barefoot because her feet hurt. Then barefoot hair-cutting was the most sensual and decadent thing Bailey had ever seen. Her rounded calves, which curved shapely up to the hemline of her old, ragged print dress, were not shaven. That dress, with the sleeves cut out, had no shape left to it, so she had a safety pin at her waist and just over her breast, exposing cleavage. Her breasts were large and pointed, seemed about to burst through the thin cloth of the dress.

"Next," the bald-headed man with the earring said, and the boy got up out of his chair as the man snapped the bib and looked at Bailey.

"I'll wait," Bailey said. The haircut was worth the wait. It was a dance, a massage, a celebration. She caressed his ears. She rubbed the hair up along his neck. She leaned over the side of Bailey's head to inspect the other side; near the corner of his eye, her breast sagged. Bent over, her body pressing against the dress, almost touching Bailey, she quivered just a bit from standing on her tiptoes. Bailey could smell her breath, the mint she had in her mouth to hide the smell of the joint she had had for lunch. He paid her with a check and, after he wrote it, circled his address, the athletic dorm.

"You're Bailey Waller, aren't you?" she said.

"Yeah," Bailey said, knowing that everybody in Austin knew the third wishbone-T quarterback who was going to take Texas to its next national championship.

That night he sneaked her into his dorm room in a

laundry sack, carried her over his shoulder like a bag of dirty laundry. He threw his roommate Pooter's mattress out in the hall and locked the door. After they drank bourbon mixed with Coke and smoked some of her dope, he felt the smooth bottoms of her feet with the sole of his bare foot, rolled next to her and felt their cool thighs touch, and he stuck his hand into her cleavage.

Then he opened his eye, and he was in Odessa with a blue-haired lady cutting his hair, and he wondered what had happened since then. But then, he thought, he had a new job. His life was about to get better.

His first day of class, Bailey had dry mouth and a headache from staying out too late the night before. He and Pooter had had a few drinks. For all his reading of the coed's history book, he had no idea what to do or say in history class, so for his first period class he stared at the uniformed twelve-year-old boys. They stared back. No doubt, Bailey thought, because they wanted to see what they aspired to be, a one-time All-American football player for the University of Texas. They all looked the same, hair cut close to their heads, white shirts, what looked like hats from an Army surplus store. Some even had gold stitching on the black brims of the hats. After fifteen minutes of staring, he told them to read the first chapter and answer the questions at the back of the book. "I'm gonna take those questions up, fellas," he told them, "and they better, by God, be right."

Second period, he didn't get to make the assignment; he fell asleep during the staring stage. He crossed his arms on his desk and laid his head against them. He closed his eyes and did not open them until a small boy who looked like a girl's doll dressed as a soldier tapped his shoulder and said, "Coach, Coach Waller, are you okay?"

"Yes," Bailey said.

The next two periods were better. Physical Education. Bailey gave the boys basketballs and locked them in the gym to play half-court while he took naps in the coaches' office. He had an hour for lunch. Then a free period when he caught more sleep. Finally, sixth period came, time for football practice.

Bailey waited in his office next to the locker room for his team to come in. The first to arrive was a skinny college kid sucking Coca-Cola from a bottle. He was doing his student teaching. As he explained to Bailey, he was the only help Bailey was to have, and he said he was glad to be working under him. He told Bailey he always wanted to play football but that he just couldn't gain weight. "Junior Williams," he said to Bailey, shifted his Coke to his left hand, stuck out his right for Bailey to shake. "Proud to meet you. Gonna be an honor working with you," Junior told him. "Oh yeah," he added, "I already gave the boys their gear. All right with you?" Junior took a swig of his Coke.

The boys, when they showed up, were tinier than Bailey had imagined. Even the little girl soldier doll who had awakened him during the second period showed up to play football. Those who could figure out that their pants had pockets for their thigh pads put them in the wrong way. Many weren't sure just how to get into hip pads. Once they were dressed, their helmets spun around their heads, their shoulder pads flapped on their shoulders.

On the practice field, Bailey saw they were as clumsy as they were small. They couldn't figure out isometric stretching exercises, so Bailey dismissed them from calisthenics and started drills to find out where his talent was. He had none. He had them run backwards and swivel their hips so he could look for a secondary; most of them fell down or tripped over one another. His quarterbacks tried to throw the football like a baseball. His running backs fumbled. His receivers had stone hands. The boys over one-hundred and fifteen pounds, his linemen, were slow and fat. Only once did Bailey feel anything good. Since no one could throw a ball, he started to toss it to the receivers. On one throw, he dropped back like he had been taught for ten years. With his arm almost naturally cocked behind his ear, and his fingers dug into the stitching on the ball, he felt his arm arching over his shoulder for the overhanded throw. He saw his wrist flipping in front of his face to give the ball spin. He saw the ball, perfect in its flight. But the good was spoiled when the ball hit a boy in the chest and knocked him down. So Bailey sent Junior long on a post pattern and heaved the ball, feeling the power in his arm and the touch in his fingers and wrist, and watched Junior drop the ball.

When he turned his attention to the linemen, Bailey realized who Bud Compton was; he was the biggest because he was the fattest. From his waist to his neck, he looked like three giant doughnuts stacked on top of one another. He was clumsy and slow. Several times during practice, he cried. "See me after practice," Bailey told him.

After practice, Bailey waited for Bud inside the cage where they hung their equipment. Junior picked up wet towels and misplaced jocks while the last stragglers finished drying and dressing, then left. Bud took his time. These boys, Bailey thought, were not football players. They were rich boys, not like black kids, not rough-necks, not electricians' or plumbers' kids, not even a few wealthy white kids who hang around with their poorer neighbors through public school education and so become football players. These boys were like their daddies; they didn't want to play football. They wanted to be engineers and accountants and lawyers. Bailey looked around at their smelly gear hanging from racks. He remembered putting on T-shirts cut off at nipple level and worn to keep shoulder pads from rubbing against skin. The rancid smelling T-shirts will stiffen from soaked-up sweat, will seem brittle, like they will shatter into pieces. He remembered the feel and the smell of shoulder pads sliding down his arms and over his head, old public school shoulder pads worn by sweating boys for at least three years so the foam padding turned hard, started to crack, no longer much cushioning left. If you made it to high school ball and became a starter, you might get new shoulder pads. And if you made it to college, you always got new shoulder pads, and you even got your T-shirt laundered every other day so that it lost the stink and stiffness. As Bailey sat in the locker room smelling the little boy sweat, he knew that these boys would never know about their equipment. These boys would never really know what Bailey remembered.

When Bud came in, Bailey led him into his office. He had Bud sit in a chair across from his desk. Bud's hair, still wet from the shower, was slicked across his scalp. His round head looked like a bloated football. Bailey looked at him hard.

"How come you're so fat, Bud?"

"My momma says it's glands," Bud said.

"Glands is an excuse, Bud," Bailey said. He looked at Bud, and Bud dropped his head. "You wanna play football, you gonna have to lose some of you."

"Yes, sir," Bud said.

"You ask your momma or maybe your daddy to help you lose weight."

"I really try, Coach," Bud said.

"Try, hell," Bailey said. "You wanna play football?"

Bud looked up at Bailey and then said, "Yes sir."

"Okay. Then you run on home and don't drink no

soda water, don't eat no junk food between here and home."

Bud turned to leave but then turned back to Bailey. He looked straight across the desk. Bailey knew that the boy was hiding some kind of great terror. "Coach, sir, I don't really want to play no football."

"What're you saying?" Bailey asked. "You don't wanna play. Why?"

"I don't like it."

"Well, Bud, why are you playing?" Bud hung his head and didn't answer. Bailey had heard some of the terror, but not all of it. He tried again. "Now, come on, you tell me why you don't wanna play no football."

Bud brought his head up and was crying, "It scares me, scares me real bad. I go home and tell my mother, and she says to quit, but then my father comes home, and he says to play football."

"So you're playing football for your daddy."

"Yes."

Bailey leaned back in his chair and thought about what it must be like to be a fat little boy who cared so little about himself that he bloats up like a three-week-dead cow. And he tried to feel the terror that showed in Bud's face.

"I just know I'm gonna get hurt," Bud whimpered, and Bailey remembered his senior year, coming back from an ankle injury, what it was like to play scared, hoping for the season to end, a new direction in his life to start, a new chance to use his potential.

"Look," Bailey said, "what you wanna tell your kids? You wanna tell 'em about your football playing days in high school, or you wanna tell 'em you grew hair and got fat?" For a moment, Bud lost his battle against crying and let tears come into his eyes, then caught himself and snorted. Bailey didn't believe what he had said and didn't really expect an answer, but he got up and closed the door to his office, then sat back down behind the desk. "You can cry if you want to," he said to Bud, but Bud shook his head and walked out of the office. Bailey watched the little stack of doughnuts go through his door and thought to himself that this boy, that all of them, should not be playing football.

He got up from his desk and walked out, intending to go home, not even putting on his street clothes. As he walked by the row of benches, he stopped to look at Junior, sitting on the last bench, sipping a Coke. "We gonna give 'em hell, huh, Coach?" Junior said. Bailey left.

The rest of the school week did not improve. Bailey had a meeting with the principal, who had been a captain in the Army. The boys called him *Commander*. Bailey couldn't judge rank by the insignia; he only knew the man was a captain by references to him at his interview and by the sign on his door. "These are good boys, Coach," Captain Mayberry began. "But as I'm sure Mr. Compton told you, they need discipline. That is why they are here, to get a better education, a more rigorous life, and more demands than in public school. They are rich boys, but they are not pampered. Things here are tight."

Bailey felt like telling the captain that he was here only to move on to something else, where there were real kids who wanted to play football and could win for themselves and for him, where he didn't have to play fat boys shaped like piled doughnuts. "Do you understand?" the captain asked.

"Yes," Bailey answered.

But Bailey didn't really understand. He knew that he was going to lose his first football game. He wasn't sure if he was going to play Bud. He had been playing Bud at center, hoping the boy would just take up so much room and look so big the defense would try to run around him. His history classes were still reading chapters and answering questions at the back of the book while he thought about the team.

The Thursday night before his Friday afternoon game, Bailey sat by his pool, drank beer, and threw his beer bottles into the pool. His landlady had left notes in his mailbox telling him not to throw beer bottles into the pool. He tore up the notes, threw them into the pool. Though he wasn't sure and couldn't explain it, he felt a terror that his life, like Bud's, was about to unravel. Maybe, he thought to himself, being only a football coach with a lousy team of boys who had no business playing, was nothing to be. He squeezed the bottle, felt the sweat of the beer. He took a long, slow sip, careful to taste the glass, to feel the bitter cold taste of the beer against the back of his throat. He wasn't sure of anything but the feeling of the beer.

But he could remember his junior year when the Longhorns fumbled away the Cotton Bowl to Notre Dame. Midway through his senior year he got hurt and had to sit on the bench, the whole time hoping he wouldn't play, and when he did play, he played only to keep from getting hurt. He sat the bench scared, and he played scared because his ankle was hurt enough to knock him out of most of a season, but not enough to keep him out. He felt he had been cheated because something was about to change his life, and he felt like hiding from it. Then, before the last game, he asked Joan to marry him.

"Jesus, think of that," Joan said. "Me marrying a genuine white, Anglo-Saxon, clean-cut, all-around jock. Guess weirder things have happened." She married him. And living with her, he found out how serious she was about becoming a lawyer who defended poor people and helped society.

Now, this night, he called her. She said she was busy. She didn't stay on the phone long, and Bailey could hear either the television or a voice in the background. Later Pooter came by.

"So tomorrow is big-time football," Pooter said.

"I'm maybe not going to go," Bailey said.

"You gotta go. You the coach, son," Pooter said. He pulled a can of beer away from the plastic that held his six-pack together. He chugged the beer, took the can in his palm, his fingertips curled over the rim of the can, his thumb against the bottom, and he slowly squeezed it until it collapsed. He held it up for Bailey to see. Bailey had seen the trick many times but he laughed anyway.

"I ain't gonna win, Pooter. Ain't no way I'm gonna win," Bailey said.

"Hell, son, you gotta lose, you gotta lose. Ain't no big deal, just like playing for TCU or Rice," Pooter said.

The humidity and clouds came just before the game. Bailey hoped the rain would wash away the field, cancel the game. In the locker room, Bailey looked over the boys. On the back row, one had his mouth wide open, let out a barely audible snore. Two others poked each other, played grab-ass. Bailey gave a pep talk. He didn't really know what he said; things that coaches usually said, things about pride and character, he supposed. Junior sat behind him, Coca-Cola in hand, cheering and yelling when he must have thought he should. Finally, the boys ran out to the field, and Bailey was up to his armpits in spinning helmets and flapping shoulder pads. Junior slapped him on the back on the way out and said, "We gonna give 'em hell, Coach."

As the game started, black thunder clouds gathered at one end of the field and gradually moved over it. Bailey watched the clouds, and he looked up into the bleachers to see Mr. Bob Compton and his pretty, well-dressed wife sitting close to the front railing, right behind Peacock's bench. Bailey watched Bob Compton push his wind-blown hair into place with the hand that wore the over-sized diamond ring and the pinkie ring.

The first two plays of the game were kickoffs, first a 6-point returned kick against Peacock Academy, second a fumbled kickoff near Peacock's own one. Peacock was lucky to recover. The third play was a safety because the middle linebacker blitzed over Bud and knocked him backward into the quarterback. Bud knocked the quarterback down in the end zone, and the linebacker jumped on him. Bailey watched as Bud got up crying. Bailey heard players on his bench curse Bud, and he knew the people in the crowd were pointing at Bud, talking about him. They didn't laugh or boo because, as Bailey knew, they respected and admired Bud's daddy.

By the second quarter, the terror that he had felt the night before came back to Bailey, and he yelled at his boys. He threw his clipboard on the ground and kicked at it. He cursed his boys, especially Bud, who would either fumble the snap or let the entire defense in over him. In the third quarter, after a boy on the other team ran through Peacock's defensive line, linebackers, and secondary, Bailey's quarterback ran up to him and asked, "Coach?" Bailey didn't answer. "What do you want us to run?"

"What do you want out of me?" Bailey asked. "What the hell you expect?" And before he could catch himself, almost happening as if it had to happen, Bailey felt himself reaching for the boy, and before he could stop himself, he grabbed the boy's shoulders and shook the boy so hard his head snapped back and forward on his neck. It was as though no boy was in that helmet and those shoulder pads. That standing uniform was just something for Bailey to shake. Then control of his body came back to him and Bailey stopped. For a moment, everyone was silent. "There," Bailey said, "it has been done," the thing that would throw his life off, twist it around. The boy was crying. The fans started to boo. Mr. Bob Compton was on his feet. Even the other team watched. Bailey turned around and saw Bud, crying still, getting off the bench to go in. "Stay there," he said. "Holstead, go in for Compton." Then Bailey went to the bench and sat down beside Bud. "You take over," he yelled to Junior.

"Huh?" Junior asked.

"You're the coach now, boy. They'll kill me."

Bailey sat out the game next to Bud. He watched the clouds and sniffed the air. He did not leave the field; he let them see him. He knew the thing that would twist his life around and hurt him was started, but was not yet finished, so he waited. When the game ended, Bailey ran to the locker room with his little boys. Just as they got into the locker room, the rain started. After the boys left, Bailey ran out the back door of the locker room to avoid Mr. Bob Compton, Captain Mayberry, and irate parents. When he got home, the telephone was ringing. He knew right away it would be somebody he did not want to talk to. The only thing he could think to do was go see Joan.

He parked across the street and ran through the rain and knocked on the door; either Joan wasn't home or wasn't answering. Bailey sat down on the porch to wait. Hot rain drops hit him in the head from a leak in the porch roof. He sat with one shoulder resting against the side of the house, his collar turned up against his neck to keep rain from running down his back, and he watched as the street turned into a shallow river and washed what used to be his front yard farther down the block.

After dark, a car he did not recognize, a BMW, pulled into the driveway. A man got out of the left side, holding a silk sport coat over his head. He ran to the right side and opened the door. He held the sport coat stretched out in both his hands over Joan's head as she got out of the car. They walked to the driveway, each holding one end of the sport coat as protection from the rain. At first, Bailey could think only of what a terrible shame it was to ruin a good sport coat, but then he saw Joan rest her cheek into the soft spot of the man's shoulder.

They didn't see Bailey when they first stepped onto the porch. The man shook his sport coat, and Joan lifted one leg behind her and slipped off a high-heeled shoe. Then she slipped off the other shoe and held both in one hand while she dug with her other hand into the purse slung over her shoulder. She pulled out her keys and stepped toward the door. Bailey stepped in front of her. She gasped, and the man quickly turned around.

"Joan," the man said.

"Jesus Christ. It's all right, I know him," Joan said.

"I'm her husband," Bailey said.

"What are you doing here?" she asked. "Why are you lurking around my house?"

"I'm not lurking."

Joan opened the door, reached inside the house, turned the porch lights on. Bailey stepped toward her, wanting to go into his house, wanting to see what she and this man had done to it, but she stood in the doorway in a way that said he could not pass. Bailey looked at her. One out-of-place strand of hair dangled in front of her face. She did not brush it away. Bailey could see she had that look that meant she was slightly drunk. He turned around to look at the man, to see what about him Joan could possibly like. He wore glasses. He was almost bald. He turned back to Joan to ask her why this guy, but instead, looked down at her bare feet.

"Jesus, Bailey," Joan said, "please leave me alone."

There was that *Jesus* again, Bailey thought.

The man stepped toward the door, but Bailey stepped and turned in front of him. "Come in, Duncan," Joan said.

"Duncan?" Bailey asked and stayed planted in front of him. Duncan had a moustache that was dripping rain.

"Bailey!" Joan said. Bailey stayed.

"It's all right, Joan, I'll just wait," Duncan said.

Bailey turned around to Joan and looked at the mascara running down her cheek, her wet hair clinging to her head. "I got to talk to you."

"Can't it wait?"

"I really fucked up."

"I'm not surprised."

"Damn it, Joan," Bailey said and stepped toward her, putting his hand out to grab her wrist, but she stepped into the doorway. He reached again but before he could put his hand around her arm, he felt Duncan's palm on his shoulder.

"I don't believe she wants to talk," Duncan said.

Bailey knew what would happen, and he knew it would feel good. It would come as a relief. It would be the final result, the culmination of all that would hurt him. He whirled around and grabbed Duncan's shirt and swung him against the house. He jerked Duncan up off his feet, and three buttons on Duncan's shirt popped off to reveal a weak chest. Duncan began slipping down the wall as Bailey held the ripping shirt, so Bailey grabbed him by the throat and lifted him until his feet were again off the ground. Bailey cocked one hand behind his ear, ready to smash Duncan's face into the wall. But then he looked at Duncan's face and watched him choking, coughing up some spittle and he heard Joan yelling at him, calling him a bastard, and he felt her slam the heel of her fist into his back. Bailey got scared because he knew that smashing Duncan's face would not help, and worse, it would not even make him feel better, and maybe worst of all, he realized it was something that did not have to happen. He let Duncan go.

Joan ran to Duncan and put her arms around him. "Get out of here! Get out of here! Damn you! Damn you!" she said to Bailey.

"I could break you in half," Bailey said to Duncan without anger, as though a question to himself and Duncan.

"I know," Duncan said through the spittle caught in his throat and mouth. "I'm sorry about starting it."

"It's okay," Bailey said. He stepped off the porch and walked to his car, no longer noticing the rain.

The rain turned into a mist within an hour. By morning it would start to evaporate, but now it made pools in the dips in the roads and made concrete slippery. Bailey was lucky he didn't wreck his car; he started drinking when he left Joan's.

He left the bars before they closed and carried a case of beer to his pool. He sat in the slow drizzle, trying to feel it against his skin, trying to taste it on his tongue. He felt the drizzle paste his hair to his forehead. He went upstairs, disconnected his telephone and gathered up all the notes that his landlady had slipped under his door warning him about throwing empties in the pool; then he threw them in the pool. Two neighbors stood on a balcony across from the pool, but he yelled at them, and they went back into their apartment. The landlady came out to evict him or call the police, but once she saw him, she just left him by the pool with his beer.

When Joan came by the pool, the mist had stopped. Bailey saw her from around the neck of his upturned bottle he was drinking from. He lowered the bottle to look at her. She had on shorts and a contrasting top.

Her legs were still in good shape, no bulges or waffle marks. Maybe her legs were even better now, Bailey thought. They were shaved. And she was barefooted. She stepped onto the wet concrete and almost slipped. She caught herself, held her arms slightly away from her body for balance, and walked carefully toward Bailey. Bailey wondered if maybe she had changed to shorts after sleeping with Duncan. He watched as she got nearer him, trying to memorize the way she looked and the way she slid on wet concrete.

"Want a beer?" Bailey asked. She shook her head, looked down at her feet, and smiled.

"Forgot my shoes," she said. She tried a new maneuver and walked with quick steps on her tiptoes to Bailey's lounge chair. Bailey hung his legs over the sides, and she sat down on the lower portion of the lounge. "Thank you," she said. "Look, Bailey," she said, "I just found out what happened to you. A friend with the paper called me. Jesus, you made the paper, Bailey. How could you?"

"Don't give me shit," Bailey said.

"Okay, okay. I came to help." Bailey looked at her, tried to see what her game was, then put his beer down and put his hand on her knee. She looked at his hand, then looked back at him.

"I couldn't possibly represent you, but I can find someone who could. And Duncan has decided not to file charges."

Bailey looked down at his hand on her knee, then back at her. "I don't want you or nobody else defending me."

"What do you want?"

He removed his hand from her knee because suddenly it seemed useless to him to have his hand on her knee. He thought about her question, trying to think of some way to tell her what it was like to be beyond wanting. "I want to know where I screwed up," he decided to say.

"Jesus, Bailey, you hit a minor," Joan said.

"You sleep with him?" Bailey asked.

Joan pressed her palm flat against her throat and chest, "I owe you nothing, Bailey, let alone an answer to that question." She stood up, and he looked at her. "What I do and with who is my business." Bailey took a sip of his beer and threw the bottle at the tube; it missed and sank. He watched the tiny wave roll toward the edge of the pool and curl up under the lip. Then he looked back up at her. She was looking at the empties in the pool. She turned to look at him.

"It is too my business," Bailey said.

"If you need legal help, call my office," Joan said and turned away from him. Bailey watched as her hips squirmed inside the shorts as she walked away from him. He saw the white half-moons of the upper backs of her thighs as the hem of her shorts rose when she walked. He knew now that he had truly lost her, she would never come back.

About midnight, the pool filling with beer bottles, Pooter came to see him. Bailey felt like vomiting the beer that had long since turned warm. He squeezed a bottle with both hands, then ran one hand up the neck of the bottle to feel the sweat on it. He took a long slow sip of beer, being careful, trying to fight against the drunkenness, to still feel the bitter but cold taste of the beer against the back of his throat. He tried to concentrate on the feel of the beer in his stomach, but all he could feel was the tight pressure of too much beer. His head was numb. His vision blurred. But he had drunk himself to a clarity of mind.

"Why you been sitting out in the rain?" Pooter asked. Bailey just looked up at him. "Hey, how much you had to drink?" Pooter asked. Bailey saw the blur of Pooter sit beside him.

"Well, hell, good time to get drunk," Pooter said.

Pooter reached into the sack that he carried and lifted out his own six-pack. Bailey heard the fizz of Pooter pulling the tab on the can, and he felt some of the spray. "Hey, hey come here, watch this. Remember, huh?" Pooter chugged the beer. Bailey didn't have to watch him because he knew what would come next. Pooter took the can in his palm, then curled his fingertips over the rim of the can. Bailey wasn't too sure of his sight, but he tried to listen. He could hear nothing but Pooter laughing.

He felt Pooter shake him and say, "Hey, how many you had?" He felt Pooter punch his shoulder. Then Pooter pulled another of his beers from the plastic. Bailey stared at the water, took another sip of beer, concentrated on tasting it. He couldn't. "My God," he thought. Then he felt the spray of Pooter's beer, heard Pooter laughing as he deliberately soaked him.

"Jesus, Bailey, son. You a couple over," Pooter said. "But not to worry, your old buddy still throwing blocks for you." Pooter started shaking him. "Wake up, son, I got you some good news. Ol' Compton come to the rescue. He ain't near as pissed as you think."

Bailey looked over at Pooter and said, "I ain't gonna win, Pooter. I ain't. No way."

"Well, the losing's over. Ain't no big deal. All you done was lose a piss-ant junior high school game, for which ain't nobody gonna give a shit nor remember. So Mr. Bob Compton gonna give you your job down at the lot right back to you, son."

Bailey closed his eyes, felt them bulging inside his head. He thought to himself, like other people his age, that just one point in a person's life is the peak, and nothing else is ever going to be quite as good. And he knew that point in his life had gone by, and he had never even noticed it.

Bailey blindly threw his beer at the pool, saw and heard the splash it made inside the inner tube. He blinked to clear his head.

"Good shot," Pooter said.

"Shit, Pooter, you just don't understand. I ain't gonna win. I had Potential. From the beginning I had it."

"That's over, son, you gotta start work tomorrow," Pooter told him.

Bailey rested his head on his knees and started to cry. Pooter patted him on the back, then just left. Bailey knew, even while he was crying, that Pooter didn't understand and couldn't excuse his crying. And he knew Pooter was right. ■

THE CASE AGAINST BILLY FEELER

When the Midland police brought Dawn Cox to the station and asked her what she knew, she started her story from the night before, with waiting for Billy Feeler at Stuckey's out on IH-20 between Midland and Odessa. She had been home for a couple of hours and gotten her boys settled down and in bed when Billy called and asked her to please, please meet him at Stuckey's. It was the first she had heard from Billy for three days, so she asked her next door neighbor, Rita, her usual sitter, to watch the boys and she drove to Stuckey's. Billy didn't sound liquored up or distraught when he called her, she told Detective Joe Sheffy and the FBI agent who told Joe Sheffy and Dawn that he was in charge of the case. Joe Sheffy wore a pretty silver-belly cowboy hat, pointy-toed black cowboy boots, and a stiffly starched powder blue shirt. The FBI agent wore a dark blue suit and pulled his gold-rimmed glasses off when he talked and put them on when he listened.

The night before, at Stuckey's, Dawn had leaned across the lunch counter on her elbows, grabbed her mug with both hands, and raised it to her mouth to blow on, then sip her hot coffee. She wrinkled her nose at the sweaty, smelly long-haul driver with the Popeye forearms who hunched over his cup of coffee and looked over at her.

Dawn knew then, as she looked at the long-haul driver, and now, as she looked at Detective Joe Sheffy, who calmly told her to take her time, that she could make herself attractive. Certain parts sagged, spread, wrinkled, as they do on most women who have had two kids and are pushing past thirty. But she always told herself she was not offensive to look at. And Dawn knew her face and body. She knew what to wear, how to fashion her hair, and how to put on makeup. Any woman her age who didn't do the best she could with what she had was a fool, Dawn figured. Joe Sheffy said "Relax," and patted her shoulder. She turned to smile at him, then turned her smile to the FBI man, who looked away from her and out the police station window.

The night-shift waitress at Stuckey's, Linda, had stood at the book rack, leafing through what was probably the sexy parts of the soap opera books. Since the only people in Stuckey's were passing through, Dawn and Billy often met there, so Dawn got to know Linda and some of the other employees. The smelly long-haul driver gave up on Dawn and swiveled on his stool to see the waitress. "Been a shooting," he said.

Linda's head swiveled around like the lunch counter stool's and said, "What?"

The long-haul driver smiled, leaned back to put his flat elbows on the lunch counter (giving Dawn a good steady whiff), and said, "Heard it on my CB. Been a shooting."

Linda put the soap opera book, now with the sexy pages dog-eared, back on the rack and walked up to the long-haul driver. "The hell you say," she said.

"Some fella found him shot in the chest over at some lumber warehouse down 20. A night watchman. He called it in, and I heard him." Linda walked to the stool on the other side of the driver and sat down. He swivelled in a complete circle to face her and away from Dawn. A woman may be desperate, Dawn thought, but she shouldn't show her desperation. But Linda was young and would learn if she didn't make too many mistakes. Dawn got up with her cup of coffee and walked to the booths that looked out the long plate glass windows to the gas pumps outside. A norther had gathered up all day, was now blowing full force. The Texaco gas sign advertising the over-priced highway gas swung violently on its hinges. The plastic cups that Stuckey's served its "to go" drinks in and several dried out tumbleweeds blew under the awning, caught for a second on the pumps, then blew out the other side of Stuckey's parking lot. The windowpane shook slightly in its sill.

Dawn thought about what she wanted to tell Joe Sheffy and the FBI agent and about what she really remembered. She told the lawmen that she sipped her coffee and looked at IH-20 out beyond Stuckey's parking lot. The FBI agent told her to get on with it, and Joe Sheffy looked meanly at the agent and told her to take her time so as to be sure to recall every detail. She did not tell them that she put the side of her face against the plate glass to follow the white stripes of IH-20. She put her forehead against the glass and exhaled, leaving a breath vapor smear on the glass, and she thought about IH-20 stretching all the way to Dallas and beyond.

She did not tell Joe Sheffy and the FBI agent how, for four long years after her first husband left her, she had worked as a waitress, just like Linda. She eventually became a night manager and moved out of her parents' house. With the oil boom and two more ex-husbands, she relied on the intelligence she always knew she had and got a job as an assistant underwriter for Houston Copeland Insurance. She advanced to be an underwriter and made enough money to support her two boys without relying on the irregular child support. With her better job, she met better people. Billy Feeler had first been her customer. He had talked to her often over the telephone about his bank's policy; then he came to Houston Copeland's office to go over a threatened suit against the bank; then he took Dawn out to lunch.

She did tell Joe Sheffy and the FBI man that the night before, as she stared down IH-20, she had seen Billy Feeler's new four-wheel drive Jeep Wagoneer pull into the gas station, and she had smiled before she ever saw him. It was a comfortable affair, she had long since decided, and she missed him. She slung her purse over her shoulder, waved bye to the waitress and the long-haul driver, and went out the front door just by the post cards. When she stepped outside, the force of the northwest wind caught her and pushed her. She jammed her hands into the pockets of her light sweater, pulled her shoulders up around her neck, and walked at a slant toward Billy's truck. She should have worn more than a sweater. This norther was a dry one and not expected to be cold this time of spring, but still the wind cut through flesh to her bones. Dawn was glad, though, that she wore jeans rather than the dress she had worn to work.

The passenger side door of the Wagoneer pushed into the wind, then slammed shut. She grabbed the car door handle with both hands and jerked the door open against the wind as Billy stretched across the seat and pushed it. Billy smiled at her when she got inside and sat down with her legs curled in her lap like an Indian. He had a new cowboy hat on, dark brown, one that she had urged him to buy. The box the hat came in lay on the console between her and Billy. She leaned across the cab and over the hat box to kiss him. He put his hand around the back of her head and pulled her against the side of his face, and she felt his whiskers burn the side of her cheek and smelled shaving lotion mixed with gasoline.

"You look like a cowboy," she said to Billy.

Billy smiled, pulled his leg up from the gas pedal to show her his shiny new boots that matched the hat. Dawn liked the way a man looked in a cowboy hat and boots. The tall, wide hats and the high heels of the boots made most men look tall, sinewy, lean, like a sleek horse. Some, Billy argued, had beer bellies that scraped across the tops of their big silver belt buckles. Dressed in the hat, boots, cleanly pressed Wrangler jeans and a stiff, starched dress shirt, most men looked to be plain, funny, but admirable men. Detective Joe Sheffy looked like this in his pressed shirt and pants, felt hat, and polished black boots. Some men looked mean dressed like a cowboy. Billy, most of the time, wore an expensive suit and dress oxfords and looked younger than forty-five. In a cowboy hat he looked older, tougher, even more distinguished to Dawn. Billy was a native of working-class Odessa, where most of the people dressed Western, but he had gone to college and moved to Midland, where he dressed like most of the other white-collar accountants and bankers, the men who were Dawn's bosses or lovers.

He pulled the cowboy hat off his head and wiped at the sweat on his forehead with his arm. He looked inside the hat. "They make you sweat," he said. Dawn looked at his wet, thinning black hair that he parted a little lower than usual to cover a growing bald spot. She reached over to him to pat his hair straight, just as she would for her boys.

"Doesn't your wife usually drive this?" she asked Billy.

"I left her the Buick," Billy said, staring straight ahead. "Where's your car?"

"Right over there," Dawn said and pointed to her '82 Capri. Billy looked at it.

"Leave it, come with me," he said.

"I've got to get home. My boys."

"Come with me," Billy had said and looked directly at her. She had thought he would start to cry.

"Well, what've you got in mind?" Dawn giggled and reached across the seat to squeeze his hand.

"No, no. I'm leaving. I'm getting out of here."

"Just like that."

"I could get up to thirty years. I can't do thirty years in prison."

"Billy," Dawn said as she squeezed his shoulder, "No one is going to convict you."

"No, you don't understand. I can't go to trial. I'm guilty. I made the loans, co-signed them, took the interest, bought my wife this car."

"You can't just run."

"The hell I can't," Billy said, trying to talk tough like the Odessa oil patch workers.

Yes, she told the FBI agent and Detective Joe Sheffy, she knew Billy was indicted for funny loans. How could she not know, she told them. The *Midland Reporter* and the TV channels were full of stories about the latest banker who got indicted. Her boss at Houston Copeland pitied the poor bankers. They made creative financial decisions when the oil boom was going and loans were easy. With the bust, the federal examiners counted the banks' money. Just all too bad, Mr. Copeland had said.

"Come with me, please be with me tonight," Billy told her.

"I have a job," Dawn said.

Billy smiled, looked like a mischievous youngster rather than a desperado. "Normal shit doesn't matter to me now."

"Matters to me," Dawn said and stared at him. "Come home with me, we'll talk."

Billy laughed like a man insulted. "No, no. If you

love me at all, you will come with me." Dawn told the two policemen exactly what he had said, but she didn't tell them that she wondered, not whether to go with Billy, but whether she loved him or not.

Dawn remembered and told Joe Sheffy and the FBI man that she got out of Billy's car and walked toward her own. Wind caught her hair and pulled it back behind her. She turned her back to the wind and felt it sweep her hair around so wildly that strands of it danced in front of her face and whipped her cheeks. Once in her car, she looked back at Billy to wave. But Billy Feeler, she remembered, jerked the gearshift to put the Wagoneer into gear and left skid marks along the slick concrete by Stuckey's gasoline pumps.

The FBI agent paced in front of Dawn. Dawn coughed from a raw tickle in her throat. The FBI agent took his glasses off, told her the case against Billy Feeler was airtight, without even a plea-bargaining hole, the kind the prosecuting attorney relished. He put his glasses on and looked at her through those glasses with the one thick lens, and she told him that was all his business. Detective Joe Sheffy told the FBI man they were just there to find out what happened and not to pester the witnesses. Dawn smiled at him and thought to reach for his hand. She looked at Joe when she told about going home.

Billy was waiting for her at her house, and they walked in together. Rita was sitting on the sofa and reading *People*. "Boys been fine," she told Dawn. Dawn trusted her, but wanted to look at her boys. She went first into Matt's room, saw him lying slantways on his bed with his sheet, bedspread, and blanket wrapped around him like a boa constrictor. He grunted and Dawn knew he was having one of those dreams boys his age have. She heard the grinding metallic sound of Matt's sole remaining hamster running in his exercise wheel. She was tempted to grab the stinky thing that she mostly fed and throw him to the cats outside. She went into Drew's room and in the darkness saw he had a pillow over his head. She tiptoed in, took the pillow off his head, and saw his thumb stuck in his mouth. "Sweet thing," she said quietly and pulled Drew's thumb out of his mouth. When he cried too much, Dawn often told Drew not to be such a titty baby. But, seeing him asleep, she saw he still was a baby.

When she came back into the living room, Billy had gathered some clothes from her room and was sticking them into a paper bag. "What the hell are you doing?" she asked and looked at Rita for an answer. Rita shrugged.

"Helping you pack," Billy said.

"Well, stop," she told him, then turned to Rita. "I'm going to take some time off. Can you get the boys dressed and off to school for me?"

"No problem," Rita said. "You gonna miss work, too?"

"Will you call in for me? Tell Mr. Copeland I had to take off. I'm sick."

"You shouldn't lie to your boss," Rita said.

Dawn walked over to Billy and hugged him. "I'll take the chance."

When the FBI man stopped her story to ask about her affair with Billy Feeler, Dawn had to stop and think. She pulled one shoe off with the toe of the other. Joe Sheffy told her sooner or later she would have to explain it. Dawn lifted her bare foot across the thigh of her other leg. She tried to say what there was to explain but didn't know how to best put it. He was married with kids, and she was not ready to be married again, so they had what people call an affair. And though they met in out-of-the-way bars or small restaurants over in Odessa, most of their good friends and his wife knew about them. When the FBI man told her that the FBI and the Midland police had talked to some of the women in her office, Joe Sheffy hung his head down, and the FBI agent put his glasses on to look directly at her.

Dawn knew that some of the women she worked with, especially the churchy married ones, gossiped about Billy Feeler and some of the past men in her life. Her looks were not enough to account for the number of men these women thought she had. And Dawn never let on except to friends about how many men she did or didn't have. Dawn remembered herself just out of high school when she married Woody Kupper. She was a country girl without religion, meaning she saw no West Texas sin in anything that broke up the boredom of living in a small West Texas town. She planned to move to the city and raise hell, or better yet, get married. Woody was going all the way to Germany with the U.S. Army. When she showed up at the church in her wedding dress and asked him how he liked it, he said he liked what was inside of it better. When he first started dating her, he liked to tell his buddies that he liked to wake up "at the crack of Dawn." When he saw her bloated and pregnant with Matt, he just left.

Dawn went back to her parents in McCamey, Texas, then moved her baby boy to Midland while she worked as a waitress. She met decent, honest Baptist Bill Cooksey. Bill pitied the still young woman with the baby boy, and married her to reform her and to have a woman younger than he to take care of him and have his children. Dawn married him because she thought comfort could replace love, thought maybe she could learn to love him. She gave it a pretty good shot and stayed married for as long as she could. She didn't have Bill's baby, though. Seven-year-old Drew was Daryl Lane's. He lived with his father for two months out of the summer. But she didn't tell any of that to

Joe Sheffy or the FBI agent. Instead, she just said she had divorced her third husband three years before when she found out he didn't like sleeping with just one woman. She told them she wasn't real lucky with men and smiled at the FBI agent, and she thought she heard Joe Sheffy giggle.

Dawn had read the *Cosmo* and *MS* articles about the importance of being a self-determined, independent woman. She could do that. She could live without money and nice presents for her and her boys. But she liked men, especially the older men she could now meet, established men with their ex-wives and families already out of their lives and minds. And she hoped she could still love. Billy Feeler was a chance.

When Joe Sheffy and the FBI man asked where she had spent the rest of the night, Dawn just told them Billy drove toward Fort Stockton and somewhere just west of it pulled off the road. She told them how he drove the Wagoneer over a rutted dirt road, then just cross-country, until he came to a stop. They spent the night in the back of the Wagoneer.

She didn't tell them how she and Billy laughed as he drove like hell toward Fort Stockton, how the wind shook the front of the Wagoneer and Billy turned up the stereo to play old music from his college days back in the mid sixties. Dawn slipped off her shoes, pulled her feet into the bucket seat, and methodically tapped time to the music on the dashboard. Billy even pulled a joint out of his glove compartment, and they smoked it. That night he was not the banker hiding from business connections and country club friends, or the cheating husband hiding from a wife, or the embezzler hiding from the bank examiners. Dawn figured he drove like hell to dare his past to catch him.

And Dawn did not tell the lawmen how she felt like she was again just graduated from high school. She forgot she had her two boys sleeping at home. She was reminded of the trip out "desert whomping," as the boy had called driving cross-country through the desert. The boy had been a friend of Woody's and hers bound for college at Texas Tech. She and the boy had given in completely to the temptation of one last fling before they changed their lives for what they had thought would be forever.

When Billy stopped the Wagoneer he took his hat off, waved it around his head, and flung it into the back of the Wagoneer. "Goddamn," he said. "I'm not going to take it. I did nothing but what I learned in college, nothing but what is standard practice. Hell, it makes sense. We all do it." Billy looked at Dawn. "I did it to take care of my family."

"I hope they appreciate it," Dawn said.

Billy laughed, reached into his sport coat and pulled out a tiny .22 pistol. "I'm not going to trial."

"Billy, don't play with that gun," Dawn said as she would talk to Matt. She wanted to laugh at Billy. He looked too innocent, and she knew him to be too timid to wave a gun around. He did not even know enough to buy a bigger gun. Dawn, who grew up with rougher people, knew the .22 was not the gun he wanted, if he was to have one. The tiny thing in his hand made him look younger than Drew. Billy put the gun on the dash of the Wagoneer. "I can't go to jail," he said, and gently bounced his head off the steering wheel of the truck. Dawn scooted over the console and dropped herself into Billy's lap. She wrapped her arms around him, and they stared at each other even though they couldn't really see much. They kissed and then climbed into the back of the Wagoneer.

They slipped out of their clothes without effort. No caught zippers or clumsy wriggling. Dawn particularly remembered feeling Billy's cool naked belly, which was expanding into middle age, on top of her own. She raised her legs as he reached behind her.

The wind shook the Wagoneer and shrieked outside of it, while they shook and shrieked inside. She did not tell Joe Sheffy or the FBI agent that it was the best night she had yet spent with Billy.

Afterwards, both of them naked under a blanket, Dawn ran her finger through the strands of hair on the top of Billy's head. He was turned sideways to her with his chest and belly pressing against her side, part of one breast caught between them, and he held her tighter than he ever had before. Dawn then told Joe Sheffy and the FBI man what Billy said, "Go with me."

"Where are you going, sweetheart?" Dawn asked.

"My kids are grown and in college. I have enough safe money to get them through. My wife can't be prosecuted. She won't miss me. I want you to go with me to Mexico, to Chihuahua City."

Dawn thought carefully about how to answer. "Matt's getting interested in girls. Drew's going to start school," she let come out of her mouth after she had thought.

"That hatbox you saw has enough cash money in it for me to support you and your kids in Chihuahua City. I speak a little Spanish and know banking well enough to get a job."

"Oh Billy, you don't know what you're asking."

"I'm asking for what will make me happy. In fact, all this may turn out to be the best that could happen to me. I'll have a new life with you," Billy pulled her closer and closer, in a gentle way, until they both cried.

"I love you," he told her just before they fell asleep. Dawn didn't know whether to tell him she loved him in return or not, so she said nothing.

The next morning, they woke too late for Billy to get the early start he wanted. As Billy folded the blanket off himself he rolled toward Dawn to look at her, and she, pretending to be asleep, knew he looked at her.

She could see him through her closed eyes. He groaned as he got up and opened the tailgate of the Wagoneer. Dawn uncoiled from the position she had slept in and watched Billy's aging body. She heard the pops his joints made and heard him bitch from sleeping on something other than his king-size Posturepedic mattress. It was hot in the back of the Wagoneer from two bodies huddled together all night. Outside, it was even hotter, but the wind was still up; it blew Billy's strands of hair straight up. She looked out the side of the Wagoneer and listened as Billy pissed next to a tire. When he climbed into the front seat and looked at the quartz clock on the dashboard, he said, "Shit, it's late."

Dawn stretched her own aging body, pushed herself up, and climbed into the bucket seat beside Billy. He looked over at her. And though she had seen his face in the morning many times before, she was shocked because the man who looked like a youngster with too many wrinkles and too little hair did not look or seem familiar. "I can't go with you, Billy," she said and hung her head down so she wouldn't have to look at him.

"I love you," Billy said again.

"And I love my two boys and can't send them to no Mexico," Dawn said and looked at him. Billy slowly nodded his head.

"I'll take you into Fort Stockton and put you on a bus back to Midland."

"You think maybe you could get me a cup of coffee first?" she asked Billy and patted the back of his head.

When the FBI agent put on his gold-rimmed glasses and asked Dawn what she left out, Joe Sheffy tried to rephrase what the agent had asked. Dawn smiled at Joe Sheffy and told him Billy Feeler never in his own mind ever believed he did anything wrong. She told them he mentioned the loans and the co-signing only once or twice to her, as he would any other lucrative business deal. When the FBI man asked again what went on the night before, she only told them about leaving Billy that morning.

Billy had stopped at Town & Country Convenience store and smiled at Dawn as he climbed out of the Wagoneer. "Thank you for coming this far," he said to her, then slammed the door behind him. She slipped off her shoe and pulled her bare foot up into the bucket seat.

As Billy Feeler wobbled toward the Town & Country in his new boots and pressed his hat to his head to steady it against the wind, Dawn watched him and thought how much she would miss him. She quickly found a stubby pencil and wrote on the back of an envelope that she loved him, that she wished she could go with him, but that she just couldn't. She wrote that she didn't want a long, tearful good-bye, so she was just leaving, she would just walk to the bus station. She asked him to please not follow her or stop her. Just as she opened the door to the Wagoneer, she saw a Fort Stockton police car turn into the convenience store parking lot, then another, then a Pecos County Deputy Sheriff's car. She said "Billy," but not loud enough so Billy could hear. Billy walked up to the convenience store's counter with two cups of coffee in his hands just as the policemen got out of their cars. Because things were happening too fast, because she had no time to think, Dawn couldn't scream or move but only watch.

When she first got to the Midland police station, Dawn had questions of her own. Joe Sheffy told her Billy Feeler's wife had not seen him for three days, worried about him, called the police. The FBI agent said he figured it out as soon as she called. He said he had seen enough white collar criminals to know that if they didn't actually try to jump bail, they sure think about it. He told her that he had people watching for Billy all the way to El Paso and in Presidio and Del Rio, said they had spotted him on the way to Fort Stockton and again that morning. The FBI agent chuckled a little bit as he told her. Dawn wondered whether Mrs. Feeler called the police because she was really worried about him or because she was jealous.

Billy didn't even see the police until they were inside the Town & Country Convenience Store. Through the windshield of the Wagoneer and through the glass of the store, Dawn could see Billy, holding the two cups of coffee in front of him, back up to the glass doors to the refrigerated soda waters. The police and deputy sheriffs calmly walked into the store, looked straight at Billy, and calmly flashed badges. Billy dropped his two cups of coffee, slipped a little in the mess he had made, and pulled his tiny .22 pistol out from his sport coat. Dawn could see him swing it around, not really pointing it at anybody. She wanted to scream at him to put the silly little gun down. The policemen all drew their guns carefully and slowly. She heard the two shots and saw Billy slam against the glass door into the refrigerated soda waters.

That's when Dawn tried to climb out of the Wagoneer and run to the store, but a Deputy Sheriff gently grabbed her arm, helped her down, and told her to stay where she was. She looked back inside the Town & Country and saw the glass doors to the soda water smeared with Billy's thick red blood. She saw the policemen walking up to him, shaking their heads. The way the policemen looked down at his body, Dawn could tell that everybody who saw it realized it was a mistake to shoot him.

Joe Sheffy politely asked if she had any more to add to her story. The FBI agent looked intently at her through his glasses, and Dawn said she figured she hadn't told them anything they didn't already know.

Reaching for his glasses, the FBI agent asked if she could tell him why Billy Feeler pulled the gun. Dawn really didn't know if she could say why, but she looked at the FBI agent and asked him if he couldn't figure out why for himself. When he put his glasses back on, Dawn told him that Billy Feeler was just scared. The FBI man nodded slowly, almost politely, and left the room.

Dawn took her foot out of her lap and slipped it back into her shoe. She stood up and turned around to look at tall Joe Sheffy in his silver-belly cowboy hat and cleanly pressed powder blue shirt. After she had spent several hours in the Fort Stockton jail, Joe Sheffy had picked her up and driven her back to Midland. She hadn't even had time to change out of her jeans and loafers and hadn't had time to call her boys. She wanted to pick Matt up from school and Drew from the day-care center. Now that she had the day off, she wanted to be with her boys and spend the afternoon and evening playing with them. Joe Sheffy offered to give her a ride home, and she accepted. He would probably call her in a day or two to see how she was, and if she was gracious enough and if she invited him, he might meet her for a lunch or a dinner later in the week.

Dawn smiled at Detective Joe Sheffy, but when he smiled back, for the first time since Billy was shot dead, she started to cry. Joe Sheffy put his hand on her shoulder and Dawn grabbed his hand; then she turned to put her face into his shoulder and wet his fresh-starched shirt with her tears. Dawn knew Joe Sheffy thought she cried for Billy Feeler. But Dawn didn't cry just because Billy Feeler was shot dead, but cried because she had made mistakes about him, and because she could not love him the way they both wanted her to. ■

A LIFE in VENICE

Monty Parker and his friends were in their booth at the Venice boardwalk selling a smuggled shipment of leather goods. Wild Jack was using his one good hand and his hook to spread out some tooled leather belts across the shelves that made up one side of their booth. Jack's woman was feeling her swollen, pregnant belly and talking to a blue-haired lady who was looking at some suitcases. Monty felt the salt-filled sea breeze slap his face, and its early morning coolness gave him a slight chill.

West Texas, the place Monty came from, didn't have cool breezes. West Texas had a cold winter wind that blew through the skin and muscles and wrapped around bones, and it had a hot summer wind that blew the moisture right out of the body. Monty looked over his shoulder at the green, gray, and blue ocean pounding its white, foamy waves against the sand. He looked ahead of him at the roller-skating path full of people on skates and bicycles and beyond that at the back of the Venice beach shacks. To his right he could see the shape of a Marina del Rey high-rise, and to his left the cliffs up toward Santa Monica.

West Texas had no color, no images. It had no trees, no shade, no natural marks, just occasional swells in the ground. It had no water, not even in the sky. Mostly, West Texas was dry, gritty hotness pushing down on people. But the heat could curl the atmosphere around into a tornado or a thunderstorm, both out to destroy anything without cover in the flat land.

Monty heard the sucking sound of Barefoot George lifting his orange-tinted, caramel soles up off the boardwalk. Monty could see the mud clots on George's kinky hair, and he could smell the wine George had drunk for breakfast. Monty watched George force the words out of his mouth while his head twitched to one side. "Harold OD'd," he said. "Man, I don't even want to touch him.

"Holy shit," Monty said and jumped over the booth and ran for their apartment. Wild Jack jumped over and ran behind him. Jack's woman and Barefoot George followed them.

Polly was waiting for them when they got to the apartment that they all shared. Monty watched her big shoulders shake and thought how silly she looked crying, her thick eye make-up turning to muddy rivers running down her cheeks. "He's dead, he's dead," she mumbled and held on to Monty's arm as he climbed the stairs to their apartment. He jerked his arm to get her hands off him and pushed open the door to their apartment.

Monty first saw several fingers curled into a claw. The dead arms were wrapped and tied with purple veins. Harold's wrists were white like the blood had stopped and forced Harold to pull his fingers into that claw. The veins in Harold's nose must have exploded, spraying the bottom part of his face and white T-shirt with tiny, almost blue specks of blood. A fly buzzed over Harold's open mouth.

Polly cried. Jack's woman cried. Then George cried. Monty and Jack pulled and stuffed Harold into a trash bag. Jack's hook tore the plastic in several places, so Monty did most of the work, with the buzzing sound of the flies in his ears.

They drove one of the canyon roads north of town, made a fire on the top of a cliff looking out on the ocean, and burned Harold. While the body was burning, they all stared into the fire and watched sizzling, evaporating slivers of plastic float off into the night. "You're not supposed to fucking die this way," Monty thought.

They drank wine and smoked dope until nightfall. While George was staring up at some stars and Polly was trying to find some light to file her nails by and Jack's woman was leaning into Jack's arms, Monty kicked the charred wood and bones and the last orange embers of Harold's fire off the cliff and into the ocean. He closed his eyes to shut out his friends and to silence the sizzling orange ember in his head.

Later that night, Monty sat in an all-night diner and drank coffee because the sizzle in his brain kept him awake. When he was fifteen, during a night without anything to do, a night like most nights in Monahans, Texas, Monty snuck back to the alley behind Slick Tom's Billiard Parlor with Melinda Sue Wengler. Monty had pushed his flat palm under the hem of Melinda Sue's skirt and along the side of her long, never shaven, bean-pole leg. As he hooked his trigger finger over the top of Melinda's panties and began to pull them down, he wondered just what he should feel, just what he would see. It was the greatest excitement he had ever had.

Melinda Sue Wengler must have also wondered just how she should feel. Maybe Melinda Sue reasoned that things that felt mysterious or different like things that looked or smelled different, like the sky before a storm, meant trouble. Or maybe the rough God of West Texas, or her God-fearing mother, whispered in her ear to keep her legs crossed. As Monty lowered her panties to her knees, Melinda Sue screamed as loud as she could.

Monty jerked up, barely getting his curled forefinger out of Melinda's panties. Monty remembered strong fingers digging into his shoulder as Melinda Sue pulled away from him. He twisted to break the grip of the fingers and saw Tom Jordan, the owner of Slick Tom's, gripping his shoulder with one hand and reaching for him with the other. He got his shoulder out of Tom's fist, but Tom caught him around the neck with his other arm. "I ain't done a thing," Monty yelled, then he saw Melinda, her skirt just below her waist, her torn panties just below her thighs, fold her arms over her face and convulse with sobbing. With his head sticking out from between Tom's hold on him, Monty was able to see Melinda curl into a tight ball, like a doodle bug, and cry and shake all over.

Later during that long West Texas night, far past midnight, when the decent folks were in bed asleep and the oil field trash roamed the downtown streets looking for some way to spend their money, Monty's mother and father slowly drove him home from the police station. They walked into the living room, and Monty pressed his back against the wall and stared at his father, hoping to see Daryl Parker's face in the street lamp shining through the living room's picture window. His mother walked through the living room and into the kitchen. In a beam of light, Monty saw his father's cracked and raw oil-field face. Monty stepped toward his father and said, "Daddy."

Then Daryl Parker raised his arm across his chest. The backhanded blow caught Monty on the side of his head and knocked him back against the wall. His knees buckled, and he slid down the wall into a sitting position, rubbed his face, and looked up at his father, whose mass of wrinkles seemed to sag. He could taste blood. He couldn't help but cry as his father bent over, gently took his elbow in one arm, and helped him to his feet. His father turned away from him, then turned back to him and said, "Now it's done. You been punished. It's over." His father slowly backed away from him and said, "Don't do that no more. Go see your mother."

When Monty walked into the kitchen, he saw his mother sitting in the dark with her hands folded on top of the kitchen table. She dipped her head toward a chair opposite her, and Monty sat down. She reached toward him to grab his hands and pulled them slowly to her until Monty's palms rested flat against her shoulders, just above her breasts, and his stomach pressed against the edge of the table. She closed her eyes and began to pray, and between the prayers, she begged Monty to pray with her.

As he had before, Monty tried repentance and prayer, but there was too much of his father in him. He couldn't get scared of the West Texas God. He didn't know in his heart that he could repent for what he had done to Melinda Sue Wengler. He didn't even understand what he had done to Melinda Sue Wengler. Monty faked a prayer as best he could and told his mother he felt better. Clara Parker pulled him across the table and folded her arms around his head, pulled him to her breast, and said, "Praise be to sweet Jesus."

Now, in the all-night diner, Monty wondered if his mother would have prayed for Harold. As the burning in his brain began to cool and give way to sleep, Monty's head started to droop toward his coffee cup. But the bell above the door of the Los Angeles coffee shop rang, and Polly walked in with a ***friend***. How easy she forgot Harold, Monty thought, as he jiggled his cup and watched the coffee swirl around in it. The cooled ember behind his eyes started to sizzle again. He set his cup down and looked up from his seat at the bar to watch the way Polly always kept some part of her body moving. He looked at her legs; she had short stubble, pink welts and brown blood clots, the results of quick and clumsy shaving, that showed through her dark hose. He looked at her lips that looked as if they were always trying to form a kiss. He looked at the guy she was with, the guy who would take Harold's place, with his hand folded back over his wrist and holding a cigarette. He stood up, yelled "You god damn silly-assed freak!" at her and left before she could answer with more than a howl.

The next morning, Monty sipped coffee that Jack's woman had made. He watched George, still asleep under the coffee table, jerking from trying to wake up without enough wine from the night before. He watched Polly come out of the bathroom, her wig on crooked, electrolyzed damaged whiskers poking out of her chin. She looked at Monty but didn't say anything.

Jack turned on the television. Phil Donahue was on. He had several AIDS victims as guests. "Why did you say that to me?" Polly asked in her scratchy, deep, early morning voice.

Monty threw his coffee cup into the TV screen. The cup hit Donahue and his AIDS victims and went through the screen, leaving a jagged-tooth grin spitting out smoke in the TV set.

"What the fuck is wrong with you?" Jack yelled and stepped toward Monty.

Jack's woman stepped in front of him and said, "Don't hurt him." Monty knew as well as she that Jack could get mean.

"I want to be normal again," Monty said.

"You're nuts," Jack said, his woman pushing him away from Monty.

Monty got out of his chair. "You're all fucking freaks or bums," he said.

Polly pulled off her wig and became Paul. "You mean me," Paul said.

"No. You're god damn queer," Monty said, "and you're all gonna end up like Harold." The last thing Monty saw when he walked out the door was George jerking as he tried to wake up.

That afternoon Monty met Wild Jack's woman. He kissed her on the cheek and then on the mouth. Because he was not sure that the baby in her belly was not his, Monty got drunk and left for Texas.

Monty felt the hot sun on his face. It was always above you, pushing down on your head, never just warm. Monty turned his head away from the sun, and with his eyes open just enough to form a slit, he looked across the scraggly, dusty flatness of West Texas toward where he thought the Davis Mountains should be. On a clear day you could see them, but not today. This kind of place needed a mean God. Los Angeles was mild. It didn't need a God.

Monty was near Pecos, Texas and riding in a cattle truck, not really minding the smells from different stages of drying cow manure and clinching his teeth against the dull ache of another hangover. He sat against the tailgate. In a corner close to him sat a wetback. The wetback's eyes were glassy and wouldn't look at anything too long; they'd just shift in his head. While Monty looked at him, the wetback reached into his back pocket and pulled out a switchblade. He flicked his wrist, and the blade locked into place. Monty looked at the Mexican's eyes. The wetback lowered his head and folded his blade into the handle, then looked up at Monty, his glassy eyes starting to water, and he snapped the blade open in front of his face.

Monty muttered "shit" to himself and looked away from the wetback. Monty had seen wetbacks like him before, flashing switchblades to hide the fear that would force them to use the knife sooner or later. After a robbery or murder, this wetback would be a real tough *pachuco*, for a while. Then he'd be dead or in jail. Monty would rather smell the cow shit than watch the wetback, but he turned his head to see the Mexican fold up his knife and put it back in his pocket. Monty closed his eyes and thought that a cattle truck was a lot like a boxcar.

When young Monty finally listened to the voices in his head, he sneaked out of Daryl's and Clara's house with a duffel bag over his shoulder and ran for the Southern Pacific tracks to a train to Pecos and El Paso. He knew nothing about hopping a train, but when he saw an open boxcar, he flung his duffel bag into it and hooked his elbows over the edge of the floor as the train gained speed. His feet got tangled, and as he slid down, he dug his fingers into the wood of the boxcar's floor and felt his fingernails rip as he slid closer and closer toward the wheels below him.

Then a pair of hands hooked under his armpits and weakly started to pull him across the boxcar floor. At first, he thought that God Himself was saving him, started to sing praise to Jesus, but then knew that the tremors shaking the hands pulling him to safety were not divine. He looked up to see a dark figure in a loose-fitting jacket and a floppy hat holding his arms and straining to back across the boxcar. When Monty's shins scraped over the edge of the floor, the man stopped pulling him and walked over to Monty's duffel bag. Monty pushed himself up and sat in a corner to watch the ragged man paw through his duffel bag. "That's mine," Monty said.

"Not too god damn grateful, are you, pup?" The man dropped the duffel bag, grunted, and dropped to his knees when the train bounced. He held his hand out to Monty. "Lucien," he said, and Monty grabbed his hand and thanked him for saving his life. "Got any liquor?" Lucien asked.

Like Lucien, Wild Jack had rescued Monty in Los Angeles. He taught Monty how to steal from Mexicans and department stores. He even made Monty his partner when he started selling hot leather goods from Mexico to tourists. Monty's first night in LA was spent in an alley next to Barefoot George. George gave Monty sips of wine. Sometime later, after they wandered to Venice, Harold and Polly let them spend several nights on the floor of their living room. Wild Jack's woman slept with Monty several times.

But now times would be better. He would go home. The proud, lily-white Jesus of Monty's mother probably never flinched when the Romans drove the nails into his wrists, but he told her that all naturally weak human beings deserved a second chance. His father would understand because he was an oilman. Being an oilman, Daryl Parker knew as much about Monty's Los Angeles friends as Clara Parker knew about her West Texas God, so he would accept what Monty had done.

Monty opened his eyes when he heard, "Hey, man," felt a tapping on his shoulder, and smelled pot. The wetback held a lit joint in front of Monty. Monty hesitated at first, then took the joint and sucked in on it. He handed it back to the wetback. They smoked three joints before they got to Monahans.

Monty banged on the back of the cab when they got close to the first Monahans exit. The driver pulled off to the side of I-20 and let Monty jump out. The wetback jumped out after him. "Where you going, man?" the wetback said.

"Monahans," Monty said.

"Me too," the wetback said.

"Not with me."

Monty turned his back to the wetback and started walking down the freeway and waved as the cattle truck passed him by. He took a glance over his shoulder and saw the wetback following him. Monty turned around. The wetback froze. "Get out of here," Monty yelled.

"Want some more dope?" the wetback asked.

"Fuck off."

Monty turned his back and walked toward the exit ramp. Walking nearly twenty yards behind Monty, the wetback followed him all the way down the exit ramp and into Monahans. "What the hell," Monty said to himself.

It was Saturday in Monahans, and Monty wandered around town looking for things to remember. His brain pushed against his skull to make the squish sound of a sponge being squeezed. The wetback walked behind him. They peered into the Sears catalog store, both their faces almost pressing against the glass. They walked across the street to Perry's Discount Five and Dime and looked at the riding lawn mowers in the front of the store. They walked another block and crossed the street to the Best Buys supermarket. Cars were pulling in and out of the parking lot, people coming out of cars and going into the store.

While Monty sat on the curb in front of the store and looked for old friends, the wetback went inside the store. Monty thought that he had lost him, but the wetback came back out of the store with an orange for each of them. Monty peeled his orange, pulled loose a slice, and bit into it. He felt the soft spray of orange juice from his bite hit him in the face. Texas was a lot hotter than California. Sweat hadn't beaded on his back and stained his shirt in California as it did on the curb of the Best Buys store in Monahans.

Monty looked back at the wetback, his orange half

peeled, and him just biting into it and tearing its insides out. “I don’t need no wetback following me all over town,” Monty said.

The wetback looked at him. The sticky orange juice clung to and knotted the thin hairs that he used for a mustache. Monty assumed from his blank look that the Mexican wouldn’t answer him and wouldn’t stop following him.

Monty closed his eyes and pressed his palms against his aching forehead. He opened his eyes to see a woman getting out of a car, a Toyota, and pulling a baby out behind her.

As she got closer, Monty watched once familiar knees slip out from under the hem of some knee-length shorts, and he admired the easy way she held the slumped baby in one cradled arm. She stepped up on the curb, forcing Monty to turn his head to see her. He could see the freckles on her forehead and cheeks that he had once teased her about. As she stepped on the rubber mat that opened the seeing-eye door, Monty calmly stood up and said, “Melinda.” She turned around smiling, but the corners of her smile dropped when she saw Monty and the wetback sitting beside him. She tightened her grip on the baby, and with her free hand, pushed the baby’s face into her shoulder and stuck her chin over the baby’s head. The automatic door swung open, she turned away from Monty and walked into Best Buys. Monty knew he had to get rid of the wetback.

Monty took the wetback to the bus station and told him to wait for him, told him that they’d catch a bus and go to Florida and pick oranges, then he went to a bar. The bar had changed since Monty was last there, a sixteen-year-old kid hanging out and hoping somebody would buy him soda water or sneak him a beer. The new owner had stuck two air-conditioners through the wall, and he moved out one pool table to make room for three blinking, shiny computer games that bleeped and yelled and otherwise annoyed the ache in Monty's head. But the same type of tough-acting kids hung out there. Kids just old enough to drink legally hugged the pinball machines with their hips. A boy with his baseball cap turned backwards on his head played pool with a friend who had an International Harvester cap on. The bartender leaned over the bar on his elbows. And, by a table in the corner, was Cow. Monty turned away from her. He put his belly against the bar and felt the edge of it with his fingers. He ran a finger around the smooth wooden hollow made by years of resting elbows, then took a sip of beer. "I know you," he heard from behind him. He turned back around.

Cow stood up and walked toward him. She was so fat that the folds of skin in her body shook when she walked. And curls of bright red hair were pasted to her forehead by sweat running down from under her stained tennis hat. Monty remembered the greasy hat and the red hair and the quivering fat. Grinning and spitting out slobber with her slurred words, Cow said, "I seen you."

"You 'member me?" she asked. "I seen you in the movies. You left for California, and you been in the movies. I seen you." She turned around and looked at the other customers.

The kid with the IH cap said, "Sure, Cow," then took a punch at the cue ball and scratched. "Shit," he said.

Monty and Petey Bates, Monty's high school best buddy, started calling her "Cow" because Petey said for two dollars she wasn't much better than one. "I don't know you," Monty said.

"Sure you do. You know me. I seen you, too." Looking around again, she said, "I seen him."

The boy with the cap turned backwards leaned against the cue, laughed at his friend's scratch, and said, "Shut up, Cow."

She looked at Monty, her grin disappearing. "You a movie star now?"

The bartender jerked up from leaning on his elbows and said, "Leave the man alone, and go drink your beer."

Monty didn't want to answer a fat, retarded woman, but after hesitating, he said, "I was an extra for a couple of days."

She smiled at Monty, and the boys playing pool and the bartender looked at him. "I knew I seen you," she said and walked back to her beer. Monty turned around and leaned over the bar, sipped his beer, and wondered if despite his hangover, he should drink enough to act drunk.

While drinking his second beer and looking at Cow smile at him, Monty suddenly was glad to have helped Cow. He wished he could have helped Lucien. Lucien and Monty had ridden the train to El Paso, and when Lucien jumped off in the El Paso train yard, Monty forgot about California and jumped out after him. As they walked beside the tracks, Lucien continued his lecture to Monty about how to be a good bum. "We're going to go to Juarez," Lucien told Monty. "This country ain't worth a good god damn anymore." Years later, Monty would know what Lucien meant. In Juarez, poverty was normal; bums could find some pride, even associate with people other than bums. But the place to beg, steal, or panhandle was across the river in El Paso.

Lucien took Monty to a whorehouse. Freddy, a black-haired, red-faced Irishman, was the pimp and manager of the **El Gallo** bar. Freddy eyed seventeen-year-old Monty and said, "No free samples, gringo."

When teenaged Consuela strutted into the bar and

smiled at Monty, Lucien said, "That's who he means." But they stayed several long months in the El Gallo, sweeping and cleaning, sometimes throwing out drunks, and Monty watched her every day.

At a liquor store in El Paso that Monty had watched from across the street, through the large window, as Lucien pointed an unloaded, rusty pistol at the store owner, Monty saw the owner give Lucien a few bills from the cash register and Lucien stuff the bills into his tattered coat pocket. Then Lucien, always the drunk, ordered two pints of bourbon. Lucien didn't slowly lower his gun and back out of the liquor store as any good stick-up man would have done, as even seventeen-year-old Monty could have guessed to do. Lucien dropped his gun hand to his side, put his gun in his coat pocket, turned his back to the owner, and ran like hell. He came out of the door of the liquor store smiling, a happy drunk, glad for his small heist. As Lucien clomped across the street in his slow gait, barely faster than walking, Monty saw the store owner appear in the doorway and raise a gun.

"Lucien," Monty screamed. Lucien just smiled and held the two bottles of bourbon out in front of him where Monty could see them. The first shot hit Lucien in the neck and the second squarely between the shoulder blades.

Lucien kept his pint bottles out in front of him as he hit his knees, and he protected the bottles as he fell face forward. Monty ran to him and grabbed the two bottles. Lucien raised his head, a knot on his forehead, and squeezed out of his blood-clogged throat, "My pocket." But Monty was too scared to grab anything other than the bottles and ran as fast as he could, stiff-legged, flat-footed in his heavy, thick-soled boots.

He ran back to the El Gallo, then ran with Consuela to a flop house in Phoenix, Arizona. When Irish Freddy caught up with them, he twisted Consuela's arm so hard that he dislocated it from her shoulder. He threatened to shoot Monty. So Monty ran to Los Angeles, where he met Wild Jack, George, Harold, and Wild Jack's woman.

Monty walked around town waiting for the day and his hangover to cool before he stepped on the front porch of his parents' house, hung his chin almost to his chest, and rang the doorbell. His mother, looking shrunken in a blue-flowered dress, answered the door. When she saw him, she put one hand to her throat, then smiled. "I thought I would drop by since I'm back," Monty said.

"Praise Jesus," she said, "I prayed you'd come back. Lord, I prayed you back." She opened the door, and as Monty stepped in, she hugged him. "Praise Jesus," she uttered again and again. Then she turned away from him and said matter-of-factly, "Dinner's ready. Clean up, Monty." His mother went into the kitchen, and Monty looked around the snug house that he barely recognized. The carpet was new, not the old rug with frayed edges. The furniture was reupholstered. His mother came back in to look at him, and he hung his head. "Praise God," she said and hugged him. Monty followed her into the kitchen. She pointed at a new gas oven. "New appliances," she said. "A wonderful thing. Praise God."

Then Daryl Parker, dressed in an undershirt, khaki pants, and an old pair of boots, came in through the back door. Monty's father had gotten fat. His belly stretched out his undershirt and hung over his pants. Loose flesh that used to be muscle hung down from his arms. He stared at Monty and stepped back as Monty stepped toward him. "I'll be," his father said, his words trailing off before he mouthed the oath.

"Daddy," Monty said and nodded his head.

"So you come back," Daryl said and looked first at

Monty and then at his wife.

"I don't know that I'll stay," Monty said. "I'm here for a while."

"I'm just glad you're back for now," Monty's mother said. "The Lord sent you." Monty looked at a shelf on one wall. On the top of it were some porcelain horses, sea shells from Aransas Pass, some knitted pot pads, a portrait of Daryl and Clara, and a Bible. Then Monty realized that he didn't remember what his home looked like.

"So what do you do for a living nowadays?" Monty asked his father and smiled.

"I got laid off," Daryl said. "Right now we're living off savings."

"Something will turn up," Clara said as she opened the door to her new gas oven. Monty's father just grunted.

At dinner, Clara prayed for Monty and thanked the Lord for sending him back. Monty sat at the head of the table across from his mother, and Clara looked at him, almost never dipping her head toward her plate. Her gaze annoyed Monty. His now flabby oilman father said nothing, and Monty poked chunks of roast beef, the best dinner he had had in years, into his mouth to keep from talking to his father. Finally, just before the Jell-O pudding dessert, Monty's father said, "So you got an earring."

"It doesn't mean anything," Monty said.

"I didn't mean that it did. Just noticed it," Daryl said.

"Men ought not wear such things," Clara said as she set tiny bowls of pudding in front of Monty and Daryl.

After dinner, Monty washed dishes as his mother dried. Often, their dripping, soapy hands brushed together so that Monty could feel the rough backs of her hands, the rising veins, and the twisted joints of her long fingers. Once, in the soapy dishwater, his mother pressed her fingertips to his palm. While they washed dishes, never really talking, Monty's father walked through the kitchen to the back yard that faced an old draw that flooded with every rain. Monty watched as his father turned sideways to creep down the sloping back yard to the drainage ditch. His mother grabbed his soapy hands in her own and led him away from the sink.

Their hands clasped together in dual prayer, Monty's mother started, "Pray to Jesus with me, Monty, and show me that you've changed." Monty closed his eyes but couldn't get a word of prayer out of his mouth. His mother sank to her knees and pulled him with her. "God sent you back. I prayed and the Lord sent you back. Now you pray with me." Monty stood slowly and gently pulled himself away from his mother. He turned his back to her and walked out the back door to his father.

He walked down the back yard slope to the draw, the sun setting in front of his eyes. Monty's father threw rocks and dirt clods toward the draw. Like all working men, Daryl Parker looked comfortable without a chair, natural in his squat, even with his belly hanging over his belt. Monty squatted beside him and threw a rock toward the draw himself. Daryl looked at him. Then slowly, pushing his hands against his knees, Daryl stood. Monty rose with him. "You saw your mother. I can't pray with her no more than you could. Matter of fact, I can't stand her praying no more."

"I know you can't, Daddy. I figured that out."

Daryl Parker looked at his son, then stuck his hands into his back pockets the way cowboys and oil-men did. "You should never have gone off," he said.

"I didn't mean to," Monty said.

"And you should never have come back."

"I got no place else."

"You just got no place, then. You can't find nothing here. Your mother's damn near lost to us now. You come back, you'll make her Jesus crazy."

"Daddy, I got nothin'," Monty said.

"And the hard truth is you got nothing here."

Monty saw his father squint, and a vein in his forehead, just under his receding hairline, filled with blood and stood out.

"I'm scared. What am I going to do?" Monty asked his father. Daryl Parker pulled his arm across his chest. And as his fleshy, flabby arm came toward Monty, Monty raised his hand, palm out, and grabbed his father's wrist before the back-handed slap could reach his face. He held on to his father's wrist and watched the loose flesh on his arm quiver. His father had tears in his eyes, but he wouldn't cry.

"I can't just whip you like I used to and be done with it," Daryl said. "Ain't much either of us can do," he said. Monty backed slowly away from him, then turned toward the house. He jerked open the screen door to the kitchen and put his hand behind him to catch it and let it bounce quietly in its frame. His mother was sleeping. She was sitting in a chair, her arms folded on the kitchen table, her head resting on her arms. She had set the chair so she could see out to the yard, but she had fallen asleep and was snoring. Monty walked straight through the house and outside.

Then, on the front porch of his parent's house, Monty's instinctual urge, the first great conviction of his life, took over again. He ran. Change and distance could erase memory. He watched one foot then the other shoot in front of him, hit the ground, pull him down the street. He kept running.

He ran until he got to the bus station. The wetback was lying across a bench. The wetback sat up when he saw Monty. Monty sat beside him, curled his back to rest his elbows on his knees, tried to suck air into his lungs, and watched drops of his sweat splatter on the bus station floor. Texas was hot and rough, every plant sticking and every rock jabbing people, sun cooking the stony scenery in summer, wind cutting into people, animals, even rocks all winter and spring. California had balmy morning breezes, not wind; cool but sunny afternoons; real mountains, not squatty mesas; and a whole white, foamy ocean bordering it, not a stinky gulf. California didn't need a rough God.

"Florida, huh?" Monty heard the wetback say. Monty breathed in and stared at the ignorant *mojado*. "Ever caught a train?" Monty asked the wetback.

"Huh?" the wetback said.

Monty said, "We can jump a train, won't cost us money."

"Florida," the wetback said, nodding his head.

"No, California," Monty said. "I got friends in California." ■

VIEJITO LOCO

Before he passed out, old feeble Casoose had been drinking from his bottle of wine and putting his box up to his throat to try to sing some half-forgotten song, something he had learned years ago picking onions and cantaloupes in Pecos. He even remembered the tunes but not the words to songs Pancho Villa's soldiers sang before they raided a town.

He woke up when the tip of some kind of stick poked his side. He was lying on a wooden park bench. He could feel the splintered wood of the bench under his stomach and pushed himself to a sitting position. He had probably gotten splinters. He opened his eyes to the faint light from the light pole that was in front of the courthouse. The nighttime had finally worn the heat away so that there was a little coolness in the air. He felt the top of his head; his hat must have fallen off, but he could not see through the darkness well enough to locate it. Next, he felt in his pocket to make sure that he still had his black box; he felt its shape and the bandana it was wrapped in. Then he saw that the stick that poked him was a billy club and was circling in front of his chest. Casoose forced his head back on his shoulders to see a black name tag with **Mike Thompson** written in white letters. He could not see the face of the policeman.

"All right, let's go, old man; you can't spend the night here." The policeman stooped and grabbed Casoose's arm. Casoose's knees cracked as his weight rose over them. Standing, he could see that the policeman was a boy with his hair cut close around his ears and on the sides of his head that showed beneath the brim of his hat.

"Take it easy," Casoose heard from another voice in front of him. He could not see who spoke. Casoose heard a car door slam. Then Deputy Sheriff Joe Sheffy stepped out of the darkness. "Hey, Mike, don't be so rough with him."

Mike Thompson's grip tightened on Casoose's arm. "We can't let him stay here," Thompson said.

"I know, I know," Deputy Joe Sheffy said.

Sheffy walked up to where Casoose could see him. He bent over and picked up Casoose's hat, straightened it, and handed it to him. "Why don't you pay your rent in advance, Casoose?"

Casoose shook his head to clear it and felt better. After all these years, the hangovers had gotten better, or had he gotten used to them. He pulled his arm against Thompson's grip. He paid his rent to Lupé González by the day. Sometimes, he did not have enough to pay the bill.

"You got that box of yours, Casoose?" Sheffy asked. Casoose patted his box. "You gonna talk to me?" Casoose shook his head, then crushed his hat, faded past any color or shape, on his head, turned his body toward the jail house. "Mike, why don't you walk ol' Casoose here on down to the jail."

"Walk, hell," Thompson said.

"Okay, you get into the car, finish my route, and I'll

walk him over."

Mike left them. Joe Sheffy placed his palm gently on Casoose's shoulder. Casoose tried to pull his shoulder out from under the hand, but it stayed on his shoulder and gently steered him toward the jail house. His knees cracked some more when he started walking. He wanted to hurry because he had to go to the toilet.

Sheffy took Casoose's forearm in both hands and helped him down from the curb. The street had little dunes of sand blown up against the curb. Sheffy held on to Casoose's arm as they crossed the street and stepped up over the next curb. Casoose had once been further east, to the valley, to pick grapefruit. There the night turned the heat of the day into little beads of moisture that clung to hair and clothes. Here, the wind picked up the hot dust, whirled it around, slapped you in the face. West Texas was a bad place for old men.

He reached into the pocket with the arm that Sheffy wasn't holding, brought out his black box and the bandana that it was wrapped in. He jerked his arm away from Sheffy to hold his black box while he mopped his face with the bandana. Then he wrapped the box back into the bandana, put it into his pocket.

When they got across the street and over the next curb, Casoose heard the slap of Sheffy's steps speed up. He walked ahead of Casoose toward an awning that overhung the drugstore. He lit a cigarette and waited Casoose to catch up. Casoose reached him just as he finished shaking his match and flipping it into the street. "Don't you have relatives, Casoose?"

Casoose shook his head. "Didn't you get to those welfare people?"

Casoose shook his head. "Couldn't you be decent enough to talk to me? You know, like human-style communication?"

Casoose shook his head.

They walked past the bakery, and Casoose stopped to press his face against the glass to look inside. Casoose used to work at the bakery. Victor Hernández gave him two dollars in the morning to help him spread the fresh pastries out behind the glass cases. At night, Victor gave him a dollar and any leftover bread if he swept up the flour in the back room. Now, Casoose wanted to catch any of the smell that might be left from the morning baking. *Buñuelos, pan dulce*, and cactus candy were spread out behind the glass under his face, but Casoose liked the cherry turnovers best. Ever since he was a boy, from the time he had gone north to pick the cherries, he liked them.

"Gonna have company tonight," Joe Sheffy said. "Got some crazy kid who shot a guy, and Rudy Armendez is drunk and cut. You know what they say, none of that movie shit, when somebody pulls a knife on you, you gonna get cut. Ain't that right?" Casoose didn't answer.

When they got to the jail, Casoose stopped and waited for Joe Sheffy to open the door and hold it open for him. "My pleasure," Joe Sheffy said as Casoose walked through the door. He went in and turned instinctively to his right, walked to the front of the jailer's desk. The desk was just two scarred tables pushed together. Piles of paper were pushed to the corners of the desk to make a clear space in the middle where a fly swatter lay. Sammy, whom Casoose knew better than Sheffy, was sitting in a swivel chair and sleeping. The back of the chair was facing the desk. He was sitting that way to catch the breeze from the rattling air conditioner anchored in the wall behind the desk.

Sheffy walked up to the desk and slammed his palm on to the top of it a couple of times. Sammy let a little breath escape from his mouth and turned slowly around and rubbed his eyes.

"Come on, Sammy," Sheffy said. "Christ, I ought to tell the sheriff."

"Just catching some sleep," Sammy said.

"What would you have done, somebody'd come breaking in or out?"

"Nobody's gonna do that."

"Sammy, come on."

Casoose tried to interrupt them by banging on the desk top. When that didn't work, he reached into his pocket for his box but decided that he didn't want to talk to the gringos. He tugged at the short sleeve of Sheffy's shirt. Sheffy looked down at him, and Casoose pointed toward the restroom behind the desk.

"Okay, go on, hurry," Sheffy said. "But you ought to ask like a decent human being."

Casoose took his time in the bathroom. He had to sit down to pee; that was the worst thing about being old. He looked at the things scratched on the wall. Most were in English now. He washed his hands several times and sloshed water onto his face and spread it through his hair. He could hear Sammy and Sheffy arguing.

When he got out of the bathroom, he saw Sheffy opening the front door and leaving through it. Sammy yelled after him, "Don't forget to close that door." Sheffy pulled the door shut behind him, and Sammy leaned back in his chair and put his hands behind his head.

"Lookee there, Casoose," Sammy said and pointed toward the air conditioner, "My son give it to us." Casoose jerked his head toward the cells. He pointed his index finger and waved it up and down. In his own private sign language this meant *hurry*, but Sammy didn't understand the sign. "Too bad for you, Casoose, it don't reach to the cells."

Casoose didn't like standing underneath the stale artificial air and talking to Sammy. He wanted to be in one of the jail cells. His legs were getting tired from holding him up, too tired.

"Say there, Casoose, you play dominoes? You stay out here a while and play some dominoes, maybe Sheffy'll come back and play too." Casoose jerked his arm violently toward the door to the cells.

"Already? Crazy Meskin. Hell, I'll do the paperwork tomorrow. Come on."

Sammy came from behind the desk. He grabbed the metal ring that held the many keys and started for the wood and iron door that led to the one big drunk room and smaller cell. Sammy pushed the door open, and Casoose followed him in.

Casoose remembered the place from the last month and the month before that and from fifty odd years ago when he first spent a night here. The peculiar smell of rancid sweat soaked into the mattresses and pillows, and the choking smell of urine-stained walls and floors never went away. Dry, crumbling plaster still fell from the ceiling. The town grew larger, then smaller again. It had new gas stations with glass walls that were broken and then repaired. It had a new bank. The jail stayed the same.

Each jail cell had a naked yellow light bulb with a string attached to its socket. Only one man was in the drunk cell. He was lying on the top of one of the bunk beds. A white handkerchief spotted with his or somebody else's blood was tied around his forehead. He had a transistor radio lying on his stomach; it was playing loud rock and roll.

"Why don't you turn that down?" Sammy said. The music grew louder as the man, who Casoose knew was named Rudy, slid his thumb down the side of the radio. "Ornery Meskin," Sammy muttered under his breath to Casoose. Sammy opened the door to the big drunk cell to let Casoose in with Rudy. Casoose had spent his last night here with Rudy, so he hesitated. Rudy was a *cabrón*. Casoose shook his head and stepped away from the cell.

"He ain't comin' in here, man," Rudy said.

"You ain't got no choice," Sammy said.

"Last time he shit his pants, man," Rudy said to Sammy. Casoose backed toward the other cell.

"He's an old man," Sammy said.

"Not in here."

"Okay, okay," Sammy said and stepped out of the cell and closed the door.

Casoose walked ahead of Sammy to the other cell and waited for him to open the door. Sammy opened the door. As Casoose went in, Sammy patted his back. Casoose stepped into the cell, heard the metal door clink shut behind him, heard Sammy mutter "Crazy Meskins" and shut the door to the office. The first time he had been in the jail, he had been in a fight with some *mojado* who got drunk in the *Terlingua Bar*, now closed. Casoose couldn't remember what the fight had been about, but remembered a woman screaming at the *mojado* to kick the shit out of him.

Casoose looked through the golden light and into the brown shadows of the cell for a place to sit or lie down. There was a toilet at the back of the cell and the bunk beds. The young prisoner was sitting on the bottom bunk, and Casoose knew that he could never climb to the top bunk. The young prisoner was staring at the floor, a cigarette in his mouth. He had no shirt on. He was tan, with taut muscles. Casoose stepped in front of him and nudged him with his forefinger.

"Mean *hombre*," Casoose heard Rudy say and laugh over the sound of the rock-and-roll music. Casoose poked him again. He needed a place to sit. The young man pulled the cigarette out from between his lips and looked up at Casoose.

"He is named Oscar, but I don't think he is no mean man. I don't think he did what they say," Rudy said. "I think he's an old woman."

Casoose looked at the young man. He motioned with his other hand for the young man to get off the lower bunk.

Oscar stood up and made a shadow that fell across Casoose. He grabbed Casoose's shoulders. Then he swung himself to one side and steered him toward the bunk. He helped Casoose into the bunk and pushed him down into it until he was lying down. "Okay, you lay down *Abuelo*," he said.

Rudy laughed from across the other cell. "*Abuelo*. Why you call a crazy old man *abuelo*?" he said. Casoose thought the same thing.

"You want to smoke?" Oscar asked. Casoose nodded and let Oscar put a Lucky Strike between his lips and light it. Casoose sucked in on the cigarette, blew the smoke out of his mouth so it mixed with the yellow light and brown shadows. Casoose couldn't afford to buy cigarettes, so he tried to enjoy this one, and he tried to enjoy the cell with its yellow light and plastered walls. The only thing ruining it was the loud music from Rudy's radio. Casoose circled his finger in the air. Oscar looked at him.

"He can't talk," Rudy said.

Casoose stuck his hand into his pocket and brought out his black box. He took the bandana from around it and put it up to his throat; he listened for his voice, "No music." Sometimes, even when he heard his voice, he was not sure it was his.

The music blared louder, and Rudy said, "Hell if I listen to him." Casoose sat up in his bunk and stared between the bars at Rudy.

"Turn it off," Oscar said.

"Shit," Rudy said and turned the radio off.

Casoose lay back down into the uneven softness of

the mattress. He took his hat off and laid it by the side of the bunk. He turned his head to see Oscar. The young man had smooth skin, no wrinkles or scars. He had thick black hair that covered his ears. He had cigarettes. Women must have liked him. He had called him *abuelo*.

The young man turned away from Casoose and walked to the window of the cell. He put his head against the bottom of the raised window and looked out between the bars at the dark outside.

Casoose returned to his cigarette and looked for the things that he knew in the cell. Directly above him was a cross carved into the plaster and stone, and next to it was a half finished face of Christ. Manuel López had done them many years ago. On the opposite wall was an ill-proportioned figure of a naked woman. Casoose had tried to scratch that figure into the wall right after Manuel López had been hanged. Casoose turned to the wall next to the bunk. He knew his eyes were not too good, but he tried to see the etchings of small letters. He could see some marks but they were no longer letters. He put his hand against the wall and felt for the letters, but they weren't letters any more, just scars in the stone. Those marks had been Spanish words that said nasty things about the gringos. His brother had carved them into the wall; he put them in Spanish so that the gringos wouldn't know what they said.

"Why do you feel a wall, *viejo*?" Casoose heard the voice of Rudy. He turned to look at him.

Rudy said, "You two should be happy. A crazy old man and an old woman." Rudy then pulled the string to his light bulb and the yellow light snapped off. Oscar then reached up and pulled the string to the light in Casoose's cell. The cell was dark, except for some light from the window. Oscar jumped into the top bunk.

"Go to sleep," he said.

In the middle of the night, Casoose felt the bunk shake and heard Oscar's heavy shoes hit the floor. He rolled on to his stomach and lifted his chin on top of his pillow and looked toward the beams of light coming in from the open window with the bars in front of it.

Oscar turned away from the window and leaned against the wall. He slid down the wall to a space on the floor next to the toilet. His chin dropped to his chest. He started to mutter something, just loud enough so that Casoose could hear but not know the words. After a few moments, he lifted his head and crossed himself.

Oscar shouldn't pray, but then gringos shouldn't put such a young man in jail. But then, the gringos always did that. Still, he shouldn't pray.

Casoose stuck his arm under him and into his pocket. He felt the damp fold of cloth and metal. He rolled over and pulled his fist from his pocket. He sat up in the bunk, and he placed the black box over the hole in his throat.

"Don't pray," he said. His voice was scratchy and it surprised him. Oscar looked up at him.

"What?"

"Don't pray," Casoose said again.

"Go to sleep."

"What good is it to pray?"

"Shut up."

"Praying is no good." Casoose tried to say more things. He let his throat relax then started to talk in Spanish.

"*Hablo poquito,*" Oscar said. "Don't speak no Spanish, so leave me alone."

Casoose tried to shift his thoughts into English. "You shouldn't pray. What good does it do? It don't help."

Oscar looked at Casoose. "What do you know,

Abuelo, huh?"

Casoose tried to force the words out of his throat, but he couldn't separate the Spanish from the English, and all that came out of his throat was some air.

"You know so much, you tell me what to do. I got to go to prison, a long time, forever maybe. The one deputy man comes in here and teases me. I had to kill a man, so now I got to go to prison."

"It isn't right to pray," Casoose said.

"Right, shit. What do you know right?"

Casoose tried to speak, but Oscar went on before he could force the air through his throat.

"My mother. *Mí madre*. She says I should go to prison. Shit. My father don't say nothing. Now I got to listen to that pig in the next cell. Shouldn't pray, huh?"

"I was in real trouble like you once," Casoose heard himself say, then took more breath for more words, "Nobody's remembered. Manual Lopez was hanged. My brother, Ignacio, was here. Three fingers, broken when the gringos try to throw him in this jail. They knew how to act."

"Shit, who cares?"

"You should learn from them."

"To hell with them."

"It is better if you don't pray."

"What does it matter? Go to sleep *Viejo*, or go to hell and take all your shit with you."

"Don't pray."

"Look *Viejo*, tell me how to get out of this, or don't tell me nothing."

Casoose pulled the little black box away from his throat, wrapped it back in the bandana, and stuck it back into his pocket. He lay down. Oscar was born at the wrong time to know about such things.

The next morning Casoose rolled out of his bunk. He saw Oscar lying along the wall, next to the toilet.

He had the blanket from his bunk spread over him. The edge of the blanket was pulled almost to the edge of his nose. A fly crawled along the side of his cheek. Casoose slowly got out of his bunk and walked to Oscar. It hurt and his knees cracked, but Casoose bent over the boy and shooed the fly away. He poked him. Casoose pulled the edge of the blanket away from the bottom of the boy's face and saw that his eyes were just half shut. He put his forefinger under the boy's nose but could feel no air. He jerked the blanket off the boy. A razor blade fell out of the folds of the blanket.

Oscar had his arms folded across his stomach, his wrists turned up. Two long gashes followed the veins up his wrists. All the blood had run out of these gashes and was now drying into dark clots on the sparse hair on Oscar's chest, staining his stomach brown.

Casoose stepped back and grabbed his black box out of his pocket. He shook the bandana away from it. He raised the box to his throat, but the noises that he made were not loud enough to wake anybody. He backed up until he hit the bars of the cell. He tried once more to shout, then dropped his black box, and shook the bars of the cell.

He heard Rudy grumble, then saw him roll over. "Shut up."

Casoose shook the bars harder.

"Goddamn, you crazy old man." Rudy sat up in bed. "Goddamn, I ever get out of here. Hey, somebody make this old man shut up."

Sammy walked through the door of the office. His eyes were red, and his hair stuck up wildly from his head. "Crazy Meskins," he said.

Sammy looked at him, and Casoose pointed toward Oscar. Sammy opened the cell door and stared. He stepped slowly toward Oscar, and Casoose pressed against the bars. Sammy inched closer to the body, stopped three feet from it, looked back at Casoose. Casoose looked back over his shoulder and saw Rudy standing with his face pressed between two bars. "Hey, what happened, man?" Rudy said. "*Que pasa, viejo*?"

Casoose turned away from the jail and walked down the street toward the courthouse. He licked the inside of his mouth with his tongue and pushed his hat on to the back of his head. The heat was already starting to bounce off the street to hit him a second time. He wanted shade. Maria Dominguez owned a small grocery at the north end of town. She would let him sit under her awning and maybe even give him some money for sweeping up.

He stopped at the bakery to smell the things there. And he looked inside at the cherry turnovers, but he knew better than to eat one; it would upset his stomach.

Casoose crossed the street to the courthouse square. From early May to late September, the old men whom Casoose had known gathered at the square, sat in the shade of the two trees that were planted thirty years ago, ate *jalapeños*, and drank beer. In November, they would pick pecans, then sit and crack them. But now there was no one left for Casoose to talk to; his friends were dead, and the new old men talked about the wrong old times. ■

THE COMMERCE STREET BRIDGE

As Georgie Chávez set his first foot into Texas mud, he said to himself that *Ignacio* was a Mexican name. His first name would be George, after the President. He grabbed weeds and the limb of a mesquite to pull himself on to the dry, hard bank, then looked behind him.

His brother, Emilio, was stuck in the river. With one hand, Emilio held the wrist of his wife Alicia and, with the other, he pressed the feet of his daughter Delores, who sat on his shoulders, against his chest. The undercurrent was sucking Alicia's feet out from under her. She tried to hold their suitcase out of the water and fought against the current. The bag she had slung around her neck dangled in the river and was pulled by the current. Emilio could do nothing but hold her up.

Georgie threw his pouch and suitcase down and jumped back into the river. He made his way to mid-stream, toward Alicia. Emilio let go of her wrist and she took an uneasy step toward Georgie. The suitcase made her lean up river; the bag around her neck pulled her down river. Georgie reached toward her as she took another step. The current pulled her under. "No," Emilio cried.

Georgie reached into the muddy water but could

feel nothing. He saw the suitcase floating farther down the river. He dove into the river and felt himself pulled. When he came up, he saw Alicia bob up ahead of him, then go under.

Now, twelve years later, Georgie Chávez walked across the Commerce Street Bridge. Sweat pasted his T-shirt to his body. His straw hat did not keep the sweat from dripping down his nose and cheeks. He blew at the bead of sweat on the tip of his nose. A bus passed him on the bridge and he smelled its fumes.

Midway across the bridge he turned east and looked at downtown San Antonio: The Tower of the Americas, the Bell Telephone Building, the Life Tower, posters, signs, billboards reading **Alamo National Bank, Frost Bros., Southwestern Bell, The San Antonio Folk Life Festival,** and **Visit the Lone Star Brewery.** When he first got to San Antonio, Georgie thought that if he could look hard enough and long enough toward the east, he could see all the way to New York. Now he was satisfied in San Antonio.

He turned and walked west. Here, he saw billboards that said, **La Cerveza Nacional de Texas: Lone Star, La Es Mejor: Budweiser,** and **Centeno 24-hr Super Market.** Smaller signs, some just hand-painted, said, **Davilla's Golden Arcade, Asar and Solomon: Pecan Shellers,** and **Rudy Mendoza's Bail Bonds.** Farther down Commerce were the ice houses (not the convenience stores with silly names) where Georgie liked to sit and drink cold beer with his buddies. Living on the west side made Georgie an American to himself.

Georgie walked four blocks down Commerce and turned south on a side street. He came to Boss's large white house, the finest in the neighborhood. Almost eighty years old, it looked new with a manicured lawn, fresh white paint, and well-trimmed hedges. It looked elegant because of the tall pecan trees in the front and back yards. Georgie walked up the long gravel and caliche driveway toward the garage. The pickup truck with the camper over its bed was half out of the garage. A stocky pair of legs stuck out from under the front of the truck; Medina slid out on his back. "Boss wants to see you," he said. Medina stood, stared at Georgie, and wiped his hands on a once-red rag faded to pink. Medina seemed to bounce on his toes and dip his shoulders even when he stood still. He was a real *pachuco*.

Georgie heard a buzz and looked over the hedges and behind him at the front yard. A newly arrived Mexican, smiling broadly, pushed a lawn mower across the lawn. He waved at Georgie. Georgie smiled and waved back. "Who's he?"

"New wetback."

"He got a family?"

"No. You better talk to Boss," Medina said. "Boss wants something." Medina stared at Georgie. Georgie stepped off the gravel and opened the gate that led into the big back yard, immediately feeling the temperature drop as he walked under the pecan trees. Even with the lawn mower buzzing, Georgie heard the whir of the cicadas. He took off his hat, pulled his handkerchief out of his pocket, and wiped the sweat off his face. He looked over his shoulder and saw Medina still looking at him.

Boss sat in an iron lawn chair in the shade of a pecan tree. He had a bucket of last fall's pecans sitting beside him, and a box filling with neatly shelled pecans. Georgie heard a pecan crack in Boss's silver nutcracker and watched as Boss gouged the meat out of the shell with a silver nut pry. As usual, Boss had his feet soaking in a plastic tub of cold water.

As Georgie got closer, Boss sloshed his feet in the water and cracked another pecan. He wore a faded and cracked felt hat that had sweat stains along the circle where the crown met the brim, a white short-sleeved shirt, and khaki work pants. Georgie looked around him. "You got another chair, Boss?" he said.

"No, guess not, Georgie," Boss said. Georgie sat in the grass and leaned against the trunk of a pecan tree. He felt cooler. He put his hat in his lap and pressed his head against the pecan tree to look up through the branches at the sky and listen to the cicadas.

"You see J.R. in the last *Dallas* show?" Boss asked him.

"You bet."

"Mean sonofabitch."

"Wish I had color TV to watch J.R. and the baseball games."

"Don't start that bitching and moaning again about what I pay you. You can afford color TV if you want to."

Georgie shrugged. "Maybe."

Boss smiled. "How's your brother doing?"

"Times are hard."

"See there. And you moan. When's he gonna come up?"

"He don't want to."

Boss shook his head, put a big pecan in his nutcracker, and slowly squeezed until he heard a sharp crack; then he began to pry the shell from the meat. "Ol' Oscar Benavides still mooching beets at Albert's?"

"Still there."

"Buy him one for me."

"Where's the dollar?"

"I'll owe you." Boss worked at his pecan. "Anyhow, I didn't ask you to come over here to talk about your financial condition or your relatives and friends. We have a problem, Georgie boy." Georgie held up his chin, wiped the top of his head with his handkerchief, then put his hat back on.

"Another batch of wetbacks come in tomorrow, and I want you to go down with Medina and pick them up," Boss continued.

"Why both of us?"

"I'm a little worried about Medina. I think that coyote fella, that Najereda boy, and Medina have something going on the side. Think maybe they got wetbacks wading across with the dope taped to their bellies."

"Medina?" Georgie asked, thinking that Medina wouldn't have the guts to cross Boss.

"Mario was raided by immigration last week. They found several wetbacks in his kitchen, but everybody knows there's wetbacks in Mario's kitchen; no news there. Anyway, these wetbacks are being deported, and a friend of a friend says they're glad they are, 'cause you see, they can come back across with some dope. Somebody has to be paying for the dope, and since most of Mario's help comes across with us . . ." Boss smiled for having figured everything out.

"You really think Medina?" Georgie chuckled to himself.

"I suspect him, and I want this dope smuggling stopped. I run a clean business. I am not about to get tangled up in dope." Boss set his nutcracker and nut pry in his lap. He looked straight at Georgie. "Now I only suspect, you understand. I'd go with him myself, but I'm too old now."

"Sure, Boss," Georgie said. "You got it. No problem."

Boss smiled and picked up his pecan cracker. He wiggled his feet in the water, then rubbed one foot with the sole of the other. "This dope has got young people thinking about nothing but money." He shook his head, then looked at Georgie, "You want to help me shell some pecans?"

Georgie stood. "No. I work for you so I don't got to shell pecans." Boss laughed, and Georgie said, "'Bye, Boss."

"You come back some time and help me shell pecans."

"No way," Georgie said over his shoulder as he walked away from Boss toward the gate. He didn't like the idea of spying on Medina. But spying was best for Boss. When he had gotten to San Antonio, most of the Mexicans he rode with looked out of the open garage door, then walked down the long caliche and gravel driveway to meet a relative or friend. But Georgie was alone, and Boss had given him a place to sleep.

As he opened the gate and stepped on the gravel, Medina came out of the garage. "What'd he say?" Medina asked.

"Nothing," Georgie said and walked past Medina. As he walked down the driveway, he heard the lawn mower and glanced at the Mexican cutting grass. They waved to each other. The new Mexican was third generation. Like the new Mexican, like Medina, Georgie started by cutting grass, then washed dishes at Mario's, then made the runs.

As he walked down the driveway, he heard the gravel crunch under his shoes and again felt the heat surround him. He remembered finding Alicia's body, a day later, floating face down in the river. She had just her underwear on because some other wetbacks had found her and stolen her clothes.

Georgie walked to Albert's Ice House. He sat on the curb under the tin awning next to old Oscar Benavides. Oscar was a tiny man whose face looked like a raisin and whose clothes were always too big for him since he found them where he could: in trash cans, at the Salvation Army thrift store, and in unguarded

Kmart aisles. He told Georgie he didn't mind being caught in Kmart. Jail wasn't that bad. They watched a few cars go down Commerce Street. "A *pelado* always does what he got to to get by, don't he, Oscar?"

"No other way. That's why he's a *pelado*," Oscar said.

They had had this discussion before, so Georgie didn't need to go on. He patted Oscar's scrawny knee and said, "*Cheve?*"

"*Si*," Oscar said and smiled at Georgie and patted his back. Georgie walked into Albert's Ice House, where there were shelves of canned goods, soap, and detergent and the frosty glass doors to the refrigerated beer, milk, and soda waters. Albert stocked everything; he even had a rack of Mexican magazines. Georgie opened the cool, sweating door to the beers and got two Lone Stars.

He took them to Joe at the crude counter, who was working today for his brother Albert, and Joe opened the beers when Georgie paid for them. He walked back outside, handed a beer to Oscar, sat beside him.

Oscar stuck the rim of the bottle to his lips and held his head back. Georgie watched as he sucked at the bottle and his Adam's apple bobbed in his throat. Oscar put the beer in his lap and said, "This one ain't cold."

"Ah, yi, yi," Georgie said, took Oscar's beer from him, and handed Oscar his beer.

"This one's a lot better."

"You got nothing better than to *chíngale* beer from people all day?"

"I sit in a truck and drive people to San Antonio. That beats working in the sun all day."

Oscar giggled, and they both took a drink. As he brought his bottle down from his lips, Georgie turned away from Oscar and saw Medina walking up the driveway. He bounced from heel to toe on each foot and dipped a shoulder at each stop. Oscar shook his head, clicked his tongue, and said, "That's a worthless *pelado*." Oscar didn't like Medina because he preached *La Raza Unida* and talked other radical shit.

Medina wore a polyester red shirt stained crimson from sweat and unbuttoned so the tails dangled behind him. Georgie could see beads of sweat on his forehead and hairless chest. He acted tough; if he didn't get shot or cut by somebody, he might eventually get as tough as old Oscar. He carried a switchblade in his back pocket, but he didn't scare Georgie.

He walked up to Oscar and Georgie. "You make money, so I ain't going to buy you no *cerveza*," Georgie said to Medina.

"I want a Coke." But Medina didn't go to get it. He sat down beside Georgie, brushed his hand through his thick, sweaty hair, folded his hands, and looked down at the ground.

"Hell of a place for a young *vato* to hang out," Oscar said and waved his hand in front of his face to shoo away some gnats. "You ought to go downtown and chase some women, huh?" Oscar said, then laughed.

"I like it here," Medina said and looked at Georgie. Georgie sipped his beer.

"Maybe I go downtown and chase the *mujeres*, huh, Oscar?" Georgie said. Medina rested his elbows on his knees.

"And maybe I go too," Oscar said and laughed.

"Shit," Medina said and got up to go inside for his Coke. When he came back, a man pulled up in a pickup. Empty paint cans in the truck's bed banged against the sides and rolled across the bed. A man Georgie knew as Bill Howard stepped out of the pickup wearing a yellow baseball cap. He walked toward them, smiling broadly.

Bill Howard nodded his head and said, "Fellas. Any of you like a job?"

Oscar laughed and said, "*Si.*"

Bill Howard laughed, then said, "Either of you other two?" Georgie shook his head no. "I've got several contracts for some roofing and some painting."

"We got jobs," Medina said.

Bill Howard smiled at him. "These are legal."

Georgie and Oscar laughed, but Medina only smiled and leaned his head back to drink his Coke, and Bill Howard stared at him. When he lowered the Coke, Medina stood straight but slumped to his left. "Eat shit, Gringo. *La Migra* know about who you hiring?"

Oscar looked scared and Georgie said, "He don't mean it. We got jobs." Bill Howard took a step back toward his truck, then said, "Your smart mouth might lose you that job." Medina shrugged. Bill Howard turned away from him, got in his pickup and drove off.

Medina smiled, "Kicked his ass."

"Why you want to start shit?" Oscar said.

"'Cause he's a *cabrón*," Medina continued. "Talking about us being illegal when he don't pay minimum wage."

"So what do you think you do?" Georgie said.

"I help my people."

Georgie laughed, then Oscar laughed.

"A hell of a lot you know," Medina said.

Georgie patted Oscar's knee and stood. "I got to catch a bus." He set his beer on the curb and walked away. Medina followed him. "You gonna catch the same bus?" Georgie asked.

"Sure, man."

When Georgie got on the bus, he said hello to the driver, walked to the back, and sat down. He liked buses. They were air-conditioned. The light shone in through the green tinted windows and made the inside shaded, yet light. The bus was empty except for him and Medina.

Medina sat across the aisle from him, then sat crossways in the seat to look at him. The bus jerked as it started; then Medina said, "Well, tell me, man, what did Boss say?"

Georgie looked at him, then closed his eyes. He and Emilio had reported the death to the Nueva Laredo police, and all they got was a free aluminum coffin. Georgie begged Emilio to let the police bury Alicia and go back across the river, but Emilio turned against the whole idea of wading the river. "*Vaya a la Monterrey*," he said.

"You know," Georgie said to Medina, "I was here only three years before I learn all the bus routes."

"So big shit. What did Boss say?"

"You ever take the express bus on the freeways and go to the malls?"

"What you talking about?"

"I like to go to the malls and watch the Anglos dressed in shorts, sandals, and sunglasses. I like to eat the ice cream they have in the malls, real ice cream, you know, not *raspas* like in Mexico. In Mexico, you eat *masa harina* until you can never shit. In the U.S.A., you eat peaches and green vegetables. America has air conditioning, color TV, plastic plants."

"Shit, *loco en la cabeza*. I asked you something."

"My brother Emilio is still in Monterrey."

"Tough shit for him. All he has to do is talk to us; we get him here."

"So why you want to *chíngale* Boss and smuggle dope?"

Medina smiled, "I say fuck him. I say you go in with me. Shit, he ain't no different than that *joto* in the truck. He don't pay you enough. Gives you a shit hook place to live. What you owe him?"

"You remember Mexico?"

"Get some *cojones*, man. No use to tell Boss and get me fired. You shut up and go in the deal with me and

Najereda; we all make one hell of a profit."

"How much profit?"

"Hell, eventually we seize the means of production."

Georgie reached up and pulled the cord to stop the bus. He stood even before the bus stopped and walked down the aisle. "Hey man. Hey," Medina said. "Hey, hey, shit, what you say?"

As he walked home, the sun set, the Gulf breeze blew in making the air cooler. After a while, fireflies replaced the gnats . . . . So Emilio, Georgie, and little Dolores had gone back up to Monterrey. Together, Georgie and Emilio made enough at the tin can factory to live on. A year later, Georgie went back to Nueva Laredo, gave Najereda $350 for a ride to San Antonio, and swam the river himself.

The wind crisscrossed between the two open windows of the cab and whipped Georgie's hair around on his head. Medina's long hair flew in front of his face. Georgie glanced out the window of the truck and saw the fields of prickly pear and mesquite trees. In this countryside, everything stung, bit, or stuck. Georgie remembered walking through it to Boss's old shack, his pant legs shredded and his arms bleeding. Georgie looked back at the road and on to the dirt road that led to the clearing. It had been a quiet ride.

Medina suddenly looked over at Georgie, "So you found your *cojones* yet? Or are you going to tell Boss?"

Georgie had spent the night thinking about money. It is important to buy microwaves, color TVs, and air-conditioners. But more important is your own good. Georgie would have liked to stay with Boss, but he could see that Medina would take Boss's business from him. "You going to have to pay to keep me quiet."

Medina smiled, "Sure man, we got lots of money."

"And you keep paying me to be quiet, and you keep me working."

Medina drummed the dash with his forefingers and bounced in his seat. "No problem, Georgie boy."

"Boss calls me Georgie boy, not you."

The brush scratched at the truck as it bounced on the rutted dirt road. Georgie drove into the clearing. Under a mesquite tree were twelve Mexican men hunkered down, their butts not touching the ground, the way poor people learn to rest. They stared at a large woman lying on the ground. A small boy held her head in his lap. Najereda stood to one side. When Georgie stopped the truck, Medina got out, and Najereda waved to him and walked toward him. Georgie opened his door, got out, then slammed the door behind him.

Najereda stopped walking, looked at Georgie, then frowned. He looked at Medina but jerked his chin toward Georgie. "He's cool," Medina said. Najereda was a short, slight man with curly black hair combed off his forehead and a thick black mustache. He limped slightly from an old gunshot wound.

"Our new pardner, *nuestro compadre*," Medina said.

Najereda smiled and stuck out his hand for Georgie to shake. Georgie shook his hand. Both his partners bragged too much, Georgie thought.

Three of the wetbacks walked up to them. Najereda looked warily at Georgie. "Okay," Medina said and motioned to the wetbacks. One at a time, the Mexicans lifted their shirts to show plastic bags taped to their stomachs. They winced, one after the other, as Medina yanked the tape off their bellies. He flipped one bag to Najereda.

Georgie walked to the mesquite tree to look at his passengers. As he got close to them, he heard the cicadas buzz and blew from his closed lips at the gnats. He hunkered with the Mexicans and swatted the gnats and flies and watched as the small boy cradled the woman's head. Her teeth were clenched, her face beaded in sweat, one leg swollen. The Mexican men watched as the boy kept the flies from her face. *"Que pasa?"* Georgie asked. Several men shrugged.

Najereda and Medina and the three dope smugglers walked to the group. Medina went to the front of the truck, lay on his back, and stuck the dope up under the fender. He came back smiling at Georgie. "Nobody gonna find no dope," he said. He stopped when he got to the group and stared at the woman.

Georgie stood and pointed at the woman. "She don't go," he said to Najereda.

Medina kneeled over her and looked at her face. *"Pinche."*

Georgie pointed at Najereda, "You get her out. She's your problem."

"She pays her money," Najereda said, "that makes her your problem." Medina stood and looked from Georgie to Najereda.

"You're pulling some shit," Georgie said to Medina.

"Honest. I don't know. She pays, she goes," Najereda said and held his hands out from his body in a lazy shrug.

Georgie stood and said to the men, "Get on, sit. Don't look out." They lined up at the truck. The boy tried to help the woman up, but Georgie held his hand over her, *"No Vaya."*

"You can't just leave her," Medina said.

"I didn't bring her," Georgie said and walked to the truck. He opened the tailgate and the door of the camper; then the Mexicans dutifully, with a practiced, orderly rush, loaded themselves on the truck.

He looked over his shoulder to see the small boy crying and jabbering in fast Spanish to the woman. Medina grabbed her under the arms, and Najereda took her knees. With the small boy running in front of them, they carried her to the truck. They got her to the truck and propped her on the tailgate. Two of the dope smugglers helped pull her inside as Najereda and Medina pushed.

"*Ella está enferma,*" one of the men said and cupped his hand over his mouth and nose.

"What's wrong with her?" Goergie asked Najereda again.

"Who knows?"

"We goddamn can't leave her here," Medina said.

"She better not cause no trouble," Georgie said to Medina, then pointed at Najereda.

"Take it easy, man," Najereda said.

When Georgie climbed into the driver's side of the cab, he gave Medina a hard glance. As he pulled the truck out, he looked in the side mirror to see Najereda waving good-bye with both hands.

As they drove over the black ranch road, the temperature neared 100 degrees. Georgie's back stuck to the vinyl seat. Medina cussed Boss for being so cheap and not buying an air conditioner or radio for the truck. Every so often, Georgie heard a low groan from the back of the truck. The Mexican woman, the men, and the boy would be hot; the bed of the truck would burn into their butts; but they would see that the ride, the trip across the river, the walk through the brush was worth it.

Boss would understand about his deal with Medina. He knew about doing what you had to. Emilio didn't. The U.S.A. is the only way, Georgie fully remembered telling Emilio when the tin can factory closed down. Neighborhood fiestas, Mass, a *cura* who came by and prayed couldn't keep you alive, he told Emilio. But Emilio stayed with Dolores in Monterrey. Now, Georgie sent him money-stuffed Christmas cards with no return address.

A man banged on the back window of the truck. "What the hell," Medina said. Georgie pushed up with the toe of his left foot and slid back up the slick, sweat-soaked vinyl seat to look through the back window. The large woman was sprawled across several of the men. Puke was on her shoulder.

"She's sick," Medina said to Georgie.

"Yeah."

"She needs to go to a hospital."

"We need for her to shut up."

"But she's sick."

"You don't think too good. How the hell we going to go to a hospital?" Georgie turned to look at Medina.

"What's with you, man? We ain't got a choice. She's got to go."

"We take her to a hospital, we lose all these guys and have to guarantee them another trip back."

"So what? It's Boss's money."

The man banged against the window. Medina turned and looked through the window. They both heard the man shout, *"Cabrones."*

A loud scream that hurt to hear came from inside the truck. Georgie, without thinking, hit the brakes and the back of the truck swerved. *"Chinga,"* Georgie said and pulled the truck off the side of the road. The woman screamed again, and two men banged on the window. Georgie turned to see the woman; her head was in the boy's lap and jerking from side to side. He looked toward Medina to see him jump out of the cab and slam the door behind him.

Georgie got out and ran to the back of the truck. Medina opened the tailgate. The stink and the heat and the buzz from the flies rolled out from the bed in a wave. Georgie and Medina pulled their heads back. *"Que pasa?"* Medina asked the boy, who held the woman's hand and babbled in Spanish. The woman was his aunt; they were making the trip alone. A snake bit her early in the morning when she wandered off to pee in the brush. The boy begged them to take her to a hospital.

Medina slammed the tailgate shut, stepped around Georgie, and walked to the driver's side of the cab. Georgie grabbed his shoulder and pulled him around. Medina reached in his back pocket and spun around with his knife in his hand. He flipped his wrist and the blade locked into place. He held the knife close to his body as Georgie had been told you should hold a knife.

"Pendejo," Georgie said and took a step back and saw a man's face pressed against the side window of the camper.

"We got to go to hospital."

"*Es estúpido.* Tough *vato.* Think. If we go to a hospital, we're both arrested and sent back to Mexico. Then we do time in Mexico 'cause you got dope under the fender."

"You want her to die?"

"They knew their chances."

"We'll drive fast for San Antonio."

Medina took another step toward the cab. "Have some *cojones*," Georgie said. "No other way." Medina folded the blade back into the handle and put the knife in his pocket. "Now let's go, and don't try no more shit," Georgie said to him. Georgie walked past him to the driver's side of the cab, got in, and looked in the rear view mirror to see Medina shut the tailgate.

When he came back into the cab, Medina looked as if he would cry. Georgie heard one of the Mexicans in the back say *"cabrón."*

He started the truck and looked at Medina. "It don't matter what those *pendejo* wetbacks say," he said to Medina. Then looking straight ahead, he said for his own good as well as for Medina's, "They gotta learn. You gotta learn. You got to have *cojones* in America." ■

A PINK HOUSE

I liked shelves in my kitchen better than cabinets 'cause you could show off your things and you ain't always closing or opening doors. I had my mother's plates with their blue-flowered edges up on one shelf. One plate had a chipped edge and another had a red line running through it which was from the fingernail polish I used to glue it back together after it cracked. People might say they're not pretty or nice dishes, but that's okay too.

I had a shiny, tan-colored electric refrigerator in my kitchen. It wasn't just an icebox like I used to have, it was a real refrigerator I bought in a good deal, second-hand, and by myself after my mother died. It had a special compartment for butter and eggs and bins for vegetables. The tan color didn't quite match my pale-blue kitchen, but I figured the little money I paid made up for its color. My kitchen isn't really painted blue but has wallpaper that my mother put up back when she first moved in. In places it peeled, and cracks in the wall underneath it ripped through in some places, but I figured that was okay, too, because I kept it real clean, always scrubbing away any dirt marks.

My butane stove wasn't too big and didn't even fill the space made for it; I always thought if I ever found as good a deal as on my refrigerator, I would buy a stove. Real nice, though, up above my stove was my shelves where I kept my cooking things and my mother's plates. My table had a linen tablecloth, which of course I always took off before I ate. It was a little torn and frayed along the edges where the lace had come undone, but I trimmed the stringy parts of it so as at least to keep it neat-looking. My mother got it for an anniversary present from my brothers even though my daddy was dead. They got it from a store in Lake Charles when they was working there. The rest of my house was not so nice as my kitchen.

The best thing about it, though, was the window looked out over my front yard. Rather than sitting on my front porch, I would lean against the window sill and watch my chickens, the shadows made by the hackberry tree in my front yard, and my day lilies, blooming or dying. I could see the road out in front of my house.

Nobody ever come down it much, but I would like to imagine who might, and I would really watch when somebody would come walking down it. When the Gulf breeze was right, I could smell and hear the oil workings from over in the bayou. Sometimes in the evenings, the breeze would blow the damp or fresh smell, depending on the time of the year, of the woods and swamp through my window.

To the one side of my house, I stored the things I collected: the oil-stained lumber that floats away from the oil drilling, the tin cans and Coca-Cola bottles I pile up and exchange for money when I got enough, the interesting or pretty things like my skunk and possum skulls, the funny-shaped driftwood, bailing and barbed wire, old metal tools, and such.

Then, one springtime, at the time my hackberry

tree and lilies was starting to bloom and turn white and purple and pretty and make the air fresh and drown out the smell of the oil workings from over in the bayou, this nigger come by.

That first day I seen him, the air had the last bit of winter left in it. He was poking around in the oil-stained lumber piled up by the side of the house. I was at my window catching some cool morning breeze and seen him wiggling this long piece of wood out from the middle of the pile. It must have taken some real big-headedness for that nigger just to walk up on my property to sniff around in my wood. I don't know what possessed me to walk outside, out to the edge of my porch, and yell at him like I did. Me without a gun or knife or even a heavy pot to swing at him. But I walked closer and saw his bigness and blackness.

"What you think you're doing?" I said.

He whirled around real fast, quicker than I ever seen a person move. Sticking out his fist, his right one, he had what looked to be a coil of wire or a barb of some sorts. He seen me; he probably seen I was just female, and he smiled and opened his big fist that turned into a pink palm. In it was this army knife with the corkscrew part stuck in between two fingers so that in a fist it would poke out of his knuckles. With his other hand, he folded the corkscrew into the pocket knife. With his thumbnail he somehow flicked the regular blade out then folded it back into the knife with his thumb.

"Get off my property," I said.

"Your property?" he said.

"I got a big dog back of my house," I said.

He chuckled a little bit. "You ain't got no dog."

I took a step back from him. He looked at me and moved closer toward me. He rested a big, bare foot on the corner of my porch. "Go away," I said.

"Why you living all by yourself here? Where's your

man?"

"When my brothers get back, I just tell them about you, they'll see you beat all to hell."

"Huh!" the nigger said real uppity. "Jesus, I ain't scared of no brothers. I been wounded twice." He pulled up one leg of his cut-off pants and showed me a shiny, long scar. He lifted his foot off the porch and turned away from me. He walked across my lily bed, all the time looking over his shoulder at me and saying, "Bye-bye, Missus."

He had a big, white, toothy grin. For a week he walked by with that grin fixed onto his face and brought the springtime wetness with him. I know he didn't have no money.

He usually passed by wearing some cut-off pants and a T-shirt all wetted down with sweat and stink. When he wasn't barefooted, slapping those big nigger soles of his onto the mud and dirt, he had on old, torn-up work boots, the kind strung up your ankles, but he didn't have no shoelaces, so the tops of them would flop around as he walked. Sometimes, he just carried those boots in his hands.

Second day that week, after a little nap, I looked out the kitchen window and seen him just standing there, waiting. He gave me a sort of lazy wave and smiled at me. That nigger grin looked like it was going to jump off his face and come running after me. I closed the burlap bags I used for curtains in front of my face.

The third day he was standing outside waiting for me to open the curtains. He had on this old muddy hat he must've found in the river. It must have one time belonged to somebody with enough money to afford it, and he tipped that muddy hat to me. Fourth day, I opened the curtains 'cause I heard this low whistling that sounded pretty. He was sitting in my front yard, his back to me. When he got up, he went into some real fancy whistling and did some kind of nigger dance out there on the front yard. As his feet came down, they slapped up little splatters of mud around his ankles. "Get out of here," I yelled at him. "Go away!"

He stopped the dance and yelled back, "Hello, Missus, how you feeling with no man?" Every day after that he said, "Hello, Missus," and I told him to go away.

The fifth day that week the weather got hot and dry, and his feet stopped making splatters of mud, but little clouds of dust, and he grew more adventuresome. He came right up to my porch and got a drink out of the hose from my pump. I caught him. He smiled that nigger grin and said he was thirsty, like he wasn't doing nothing wrong, like he was a part of the place.

The sixth day, I looked out my window, and he wasn't there. I went into the yard, couldn't see him nowhere. I went out to the pump, and this big finger tapped me on the shoulder from behind. I whirled around to slap at that black face I knew was there, but missed it.

He started to laugh, a deep, man laugh. He stamped his feet on the ground, making a slapping sound when he threw them down and lifted them up. "I fooled you," he said. I almost laughed, too, but I didn't.

When he was through laughing he came up to me. He had his shoes strung together by a string hanging around his shoulders, one shoe up against each of his cheeks. He had the nigger-man smell about him, so sweet it stinks. It was the closest I had seen him. His eyes had red veins at the corners that made him look troubled and mean. What little hair he had on his chest was curled like the corkscrew on his knife. On his arms and shoulders, his skin had white, powdery flecks. "Ain't no reason I can't have that wood," he said, "or that shed," pointing to my shack that I used for a tool house. I looked at his thick wrist with its round, brown veins.

"It ain't yours."

"You let me have that wood, and I'll build that shed up for you."

"No. I don't need that shed."

"Good, I'll build it up and stay there."

"You can't stay there. What the hell you think this is?"

"We'll talk about it when I do it."

"You can't be here," I yelled at him, "Now get, go away!"

"Why?" he said.

That nigger thinking there was no wrong with him staying right up against me. I wondered what kind of man he might be, willing to stay in a crumbling old shed. Probably trash of the worst kind. I told him to go away and never come back. He walked off, but the next day, last day of the week, about the first of April, he came back and asked me again. A kind of cool drizzle was falling, and he hunched his shoulders against his neck as he walked through it, and I said yes. Said he could stay for a while but he had to leave just when I said so. When I told him, he raised his head up and sort of waved it and said, "You got yourself a fine man, Missus."

"You ain't my man," I said.

He laughed, then said, "How you make your money out here all by yourself?"

"My dead mother left me land I can lease out. Do the bookkeeping myself."

"My name is Julius," he said and stuck out his hand for me to shake, but I didn't.

So Julius become my nigger. Next day, he come back with a saw and a hammer. I stayed inside my kitchen and sat by my table, not wanting to look out my window and be nosy, but I couldn't keep from it. He wasn't there. So I snuck outside to look at the woodpile he had made a few dents in. He hadn't done nothing. That shed was not fit for any kind of decent human being. It had holes in the walls and the roof, and the wood in places was so rotten it just crumbled into splinters.

That night, making sure I had no lights but what I needed turned on in my house, I smelled cooking outside. I hurried to my window and looked out. He had a fire going beside the shed, roasting a skewered chicken. I turned around when he looked toward my window. I went out on my front porch and looked across the yard at him. Squatting on his haunches, he pulled the chicken in from the fire and, hardly waiting for it to cool, held it careful and pulled the skewer out; then he saw me and smiled. He shifted his feet so I couldn't see him too good. I stepped off the porch to see him better. Shifting his feet some more, he got himself situated to where we could see each other. He took that hot chicken in his hand, rubbed his hands across the greasy breast bone. Then he jerked quick on it and half of the chicken tore away from the other. He set half the chicken down on a board and tore off a part of the other. Then smiling at me, he stuck some of that part in his mouth and started chewing. I could swear I heard chicken bones popping and breaking, like he was chewing the whole thing up, bones and all. I turned to go back to my meal, and I heard, "Thank you, Missus." I counted my chickens.

He ate like that all the time. Just gobble up anything set in front of him. Suck it right down his throat. Once he brought home a six-pack of soda waters. He pulled the cap off a bottle of soda with his teeth, then spit it out his mouth. He drank the soda, had his head thrown back and the bottle sticking straight up out of his mouth. That grape soda bubbled in the bottle before it slid into his mouth. When he was through sucking the bottle dry, he threw it on the ground.

And he did funny things. One afternoon, when the sun shone real nice, he took a break from working, slid his T-shirt off over his head, and sat on my front porch. I walked out the front door, not knowing what I was going to say. When I got to the door, I just looked out the screen and saw him pull some dice from his pocket. He closed his fist over both of them and cocked it up around his ear. He threw the dice down on my porch. They rolled across it and bounced off the wall of the house. One die rolled up five and the other one two. He smiled, then stretched across the porch, half laying on it, and scooped up the dice. He rolled them again, and the same numbers popped up. He stretched to grab them and I said, "What you doing?"

He said, "Practicing." Then he got up to go back to work, sticking his dice back in his pocket.

Another time, at night, I heard him whistling, not the fancy, nigger-type whistling I heard from him before, but pretty whistling that made you sad. Every once in a while, between his whistling, he would sing out, kinda low, what I knew was French from listening to Cajuns when I went to Baton Rouge with my mother.

I came out on my little porch, out to the edge of it, listening to that music he was making, watching for him to walk past his lit window. I started to walk toward his shed. I wanted to see him whistling, and I wanted to tell him get out, go away. And I don't know why I did, but I just pushed the door open and looked at him. He was laying on an army cot. It was the only thing in the shed. Some candles circling the cot set his dark colors dancing on his face. He was singing, never noticing me, his hands folded across his belly.

"You got to go," I said.

He reached under the cot and drug one of his boots

out from under it. Real quick, he just flung the boot toward me. It hit the door almost even to my head, and little pieces of caked mud from the heel of the boot hit my face. I jerked the door closed and ran back to my house, his singing following me all the way back, into my locked bedroom, and through the pillow I held over my head and ears.

Mostly, he built up his shed. I heard the buzzing sound of his work most of the day. He brought in more boards and lumber he must have found in the river or alongside the road. Some of it even looked like it had been fresh cut, from a lumber yard somewhere, but I knew he couldn't buy no wood from a lumber yard. His shed grew, but it had gaps in it where air could blow through, gaps where he couldn't find no boards the right size to plug them.

Nights he usually left and didn't come back until I was asleep. Sometimes, when I rested on my porch in the Gulf breeze, he would ask me if there was anything I needed, like as though he had money. I don't know where he went, never said I wanted anything, but he always came back with something.

One morning, he brought back two cans of paint. He opened them and mixed them up. I went out into the yard to see what he was doing. He dumped a little paint from one can into the other one and shook it up a little. He stirred his new color with a stick. When he began painting, I saw his paint was pink. "What you doing spreading that awful color on my shed?" I said.

He turned around to look at me and said, "It's my paint," and I said nothing. And I said nothing when he showed up with some curtains, nice green ones that caught the sunlight real nice. I thought he might have brought them home as a present for me so I could get rid of my burlap bag curtains, but he went inside his shed and hammered until those curtains were hanging in his one window. Those curtains sure did show up against the pink paint.

He started planting things, too, flowers I never seen. They were pretty and smelled nicer than mine. He put in peas and onions in his little garden. After a while his place started to look like a real house.

I watched him working or painting or planting through my kitchen window. I looked at the way his purple-dark body reflected sunlight in a certain way that made him shine. The way his muscles moved around in his shoulders and back when he stooped or lifted made me think of flour shifting in a sack. He was almost what could be called right handsome for a nigger. At night, I looked at the lit window of his shack and saw the flickering shadows behind him walking around.

And I thought about the day I let him stay and he stuck out his hand for me to shake. I remember the big round veins in his wrists. To me, they looked like the thick middle branches of my hackberry tree. My own wrists were thin, all white, like my mother's, the veins just barely blue lines showing through the skin. My brother Irwin's wrists were just like mine, too thin. My other brother, Henry, had big, rounded veins in rough, thick wrists. He was big, but he was ugly and full of meanness, left my mother and me to work in Houston. Irwin was a nice boy but was killed in an accident on the river.

Toward the beginning of summer, I killed one of my best chickens for dinner, a big, plump chicken. I wrung its neck, let the blood drain out, boiled it to pluck out the feathers. For cooking, I smeared it with butter, then baked it real slow to let the grease mix in with the meat and make it all taste better. I put lots of pepper on it to make it taste better. I cut off a leg and wing for me and cut up the rest for Julius, so he wouldn't have to tear it apart.

I walked toward the light of his shed, plate of

chicken in my hand, wanting to see how he lived, and I wanted to see the inside of his pink house, what he had done to it with all his working. I knocked on the door, but he didn't answer. I yelled out, "You," but I only heard him grumble. I didn't really want to go in. I shouldn't have, but I did go in.

The house, so pretty on the outside, had just half a floor, and that was just made out of bricks and bits of wood stuck in the dirt. The only furniture he had was one table sitting back from the front door, a crate pulled up to it like a chair, and his army cot. He was sitting in one corner, leaning up against the wall. One long, tilting candle burned in the middle of the floor. His breathing wheezed. "You all right?" I said. I could just barely see his head nod. I stepped in and walked closer to him. "I got supper for you," I said.

"Leave it," he said.

I set the plate of chicken down next to the candle, and I started to go, but I got curious and picked up the candle and held it out in front of me so I could see him. "What's wrong with you?" I said. He rolled his head away from the light, but I could still see that one eye was puffy and swelled.

"Take it away," he said.

"What's wrong with your eyes?"

I kneeled beside him and held the candle in front of his face. I couldn't even see any of his eyeball, and his cheek looked like rising dough, and a trickle of blood had run out his nose and was drying on his upper lip. I bunched up a little of my apron and dabbed it at the tip of my tongue and wiped off that little bit of blood. He groaned. "Can you eat?" I asked him.

"Maybe," he said. I reached behind me and grabbed the plate of chicken and stuck it in front of him. He put his hands on his cheeks and jaws and rubbed them like he was loosening up his chewing muscles. He picked up a drumstick and stuck the end of it in his mouth. He didn't chew. I could tell from the way his cheeks bulged that he was sucking the meat off the bone, kind of mashing it up by scraping it against his teeth with his tongue. He took a hard swallow, then set the drumstick back on the plate. "Thank you," he said, then closed his eyes.

I left him and ran back into my house. I sat at my kitchen table, trying to eat. I prayed to God to make that nigger Julius leave.

Morning, two days later, was hotter than most. It had rained during the night. The dripping and clatter of rain on my tin roof kept me up. With the morning sunshine, all that wetness got mixed up in the air. I got up and rubbed and pulled my sweat-soaked hair. I pulled it together in a knot at the back of my head, then lifted it over a shoulder to hang by my cheek. The first sounds of the morning were animal sounds, crows, rooster and chickens, a yelping dog. The smell was supposed to be cleaner, the rain was supposed to do that, make things smell fresh, but this rain that came and went through several days filled up the air with oil smell and its sticky feel.

I looked out my window at Julius' shed. The drizzle made everything look thick and gray, but the pink house stood out. I went to the front door, thinking I might take a dip in the cool part of the bayou. I pushed open the screen door to the porch. He was there. He was on my porch, laying with nothing but a wet blanket over him, still half-asleep. He rolled over on his back and looked up at me. His eye was still a little puffy.

"You here? What you doing here?" I said. He straightened his arm and folded the blanket off him. He got up, and I saw he had no shirt on, little beads of wet rolled down his chest, and he shook from being hot then cold all night.

"My roof leaks," he said.

"You're wet," I said, "and shaking."

"Yeah."

"Why don't you come in? I'll give you breakfast, maybe a towel. Then you got to get." He followed me in through the screen door, not holding a hand or shoulder behind him to catch it and let it close into place gentle, but letting it slam into the frame and bounce.

We walked through the living room to the kitchen. I pointed to a chair by the table. "Sit down," I said. He sat down at the table, looking at me, then shifting his head around the room. He looked at the burlap bags that hung for curtains over my kitchen window. He looked at my refrigerator. He had no right to be sniffing over my house like he was. I walked to the refrigerator, opened it real wide to show him I had food in it, and reached into it with both hands to bring out two eggs. They were all the eggs I had.

He got up and still shaking walked to the doorway into the living room. He rolled his head around on his shoulders and looked at the living room just the way he did at my kitchen. I put my frying pan on the burner of my butane stove and poured a little leftover bacon grease into the pan. "What you doing? Sit down here, or you ain't getting any breakfast."

I turned my body but not my head toward the stove; then I said, "It ain't your place."

I broke one egg shell and dumped the egg into the pan and watched the grease bubble and spurt and then dumped the other egg in. I looked over my shoulder at him, sitting at my table, tapping his finger, looking at my kitchen. I looked at my frying eggs. Sliding my spatula under the first egg, I lifted one end of it, shook the spatula, and got it all the way under the egg; eggs taste and look so much better when you flip them right. I went for the other egg, got it up on the spatula and said to him, "You got to leave today." The egg fell off the spatula and back into the pan, breaking the yoke. I turned around to look at him, just sitting at that table, not paying me any mind. "You hear me?"

"Yeah," he said.

I picked up the frying pan, forgetting how hot the handle would be. I yelled a little and dropped the pan. I was blowing into the palm of my hand and shaking it, and he got up from the table like he was going to help me. "Sit down, I'll do it," I said. He sat back down. I grabbed the handle of the frying pan with a bunched up part of my skirt, shook the pan, and worked the eggs with the spatula onto a plate.

I thought about giving him both eggs, but I wasn't going to do that now, so I got another plate and slid the unbroke egg onto it with the spatula. He looked at me as I walked to the table and put the unbroke egg in front of him. He smiled at me, almost like he was going to say thank you, then looked at his egg like it was pitiful. Grabbing the plate with the egg in it, he brought it to his mouth, rested the edge of the plate on his bottom lip, and tipped the plate up. The egg slid into his mouth and down his gullet. "Thank you. It was good," he said.

Damn him. Damn him for doing that, reminding me how little it was I give him, how little my house was, how bright his house was. Damn him. I wanted to tell him, but could only look at him sitting in front of me, still shaking a little from that chill. His shoulders were heaving, his hands shaking, his chest dripping with rain and sweat. "You want a towel?" I asked. He shook his head, but I bunched up my skirt and began to dry off his head.

He turned as I rubbed him, and stood up. My hands, wrapped in my skirt, scraped across his face, then down his neck to his chest. He was standing in front of me, shiny, purple-dark all over with rain running down his almost hairless chest, and smelling strong like nigger sweat, sour and sweet. I rubbed him with my skirt, gentle, then harder. I felt him shake just a little. Then I felt his hand on my waist. His gentle hand was pulling me into him, pulling me into that blackness, and I wanted to crawl inside that blackness, get up against it, have it all around me and rubbing off on me.

I looked up into his face, and I saw the big drops of sweat rolling off his cheeks. I could feel the sting of his sweat, I could taste it. I closed my eyes so I could not see him, and I couldn't see my kitchen. ■

LADIES' MAN

I know about certain women. I can spot them. They have kids between six and sixteen. If the kids are just starting school, the moms finally have some peace and quiet for themselves or, if they have *careers*, they feel some ease at having gotten the kids to school age without screwing them up too badly. On the teen side of childhood, if the kids are close to becoming independent adults, going off to college, becoming drug addicts, joining the army, or remaining a burden to their parents, their moms feel much easier because, no matter how promising or screwed up, their babies are now beyond them. In either position, Mom looks at her life and decides she needs some excitement that she lost in her past. Which is where I come in.

I can spot them coming into the **Ginger Man**, a decent fern bar that purposely tries to keep the head-banging younger drinkers out in order to attract some older drinkers with more money and less destructive personalities. Mark Hightower, manager of the Ginger Man, keeps the lights up, the music low, so people can talk. It is the sort of clean, well-lighted place with just a scent of risk in the air that settled women like. The moms come in with other moms, smiling at each other, but glancing around the place to try to spot some man other than their husband. They dip their heads, like shy co-eds, when an obnoxious man comes up to them, but if they think they might take a chance with him, they'll forget the manners their Southern mamas taught them and look the man straight in the eye.

They've seen their bodies change, spread out, sag, wrinkle, wither, so they take advantage of their advantages: the drape of their skirts over the curves of their butts, the proportions between thigh and calf, the tightness of jeans, the way hollowed cheeks or loosening jowls catch the light or the shadows. No twenty-year-old *Playboy* centerfold could match the beauty of these women. I like women who look better in their clothes than out of them.

My type of women can spot an obvious pick-up line; they're old enough to have heard a few. I can't just buy them a drink, ask about their astrological sign, invite them to dance. I have to first get lucky enough for them to sit near me, then I have to pick up some piece of their conversation, and then at the right moment, I have to add something to the discussion. Because I am clean, am modestly but neatly dressed, talk without a discernible Texas accent, am not offensive to look at, they will usually listen to me. In college, I wisely studied literature, for my study of literature made me a better bullshitter, a more appropriate term for a conversationalist, and really, bullshitting helps a man meet these women.

Younger unmarried or never-married women would never listen to me. I am not young enough or handsome enough for them. They do not know enough about misery or desperation or just the uneasiness that comes with the ease and security of marriage to gamble that I might be more than another lounge lizard with a hyperactive crotch.

Of course, you can accuse me of being what some young women call a ***horny toad***, but most womanizers don't love these women as much as I do. To just watch them, see them glide across the floor of the Ginger Man up to the bar is enough; it makes the night. Repeated ***hellos***, hustling for some conversation, maybe becoming friends makes me look forward to my visits to the Ginger Man. Becoming involved with ***one of them***, seeing ***one of them***, is ecstasy, too much to ask for, the greatest excitement in life.

That first night together is mysterious, but a bit clumsy. The second, third, fourth nights are better because the mystery is still there but not the lame clumsiness; these are the best nights for a horny toad who really appreciates women. Unfortunately, somewhere shortly after the height of this excitement, after they realize that they don't love me or are too scared to love me, they usually focus their attentions back on their husbands or ex-husbands or boyfriends. Which is my point: none of us can ever satisfy the excitement that we help arouse in another. Just as well; I want to *see* them all.

I know about that persistent itch for excitement. I remember my marriage. Mostly I remember sitting in my easy chair in front of my TV set and looking down at my growing gut. I was happy with Donna, nothing to complain about. A great wife. I could even find her attractive if she walked into the Ginger Man, because, no doubt, she would have looked like the women I love. I made good money. Studying literature and picking up the ability to bullshit also enabled me to convince an investment company that I could be a salesman. With an economics and a business textbook and some in-house training, I began getting sweet contracts from college professors and mid-level businessmen for retirement programs. I landed twenty gorillas,

$100,000 or over accounts, in one month, a company record. Donna made decent money as a junior high P.E. instructor. We lived in a townhouse in the good part of Houston, drove matching Toyotas, talked about kids. We were comfortable, secure. Which is to say, we had a habit. Habit is fine; it is as seductive as excitement, but I missed excitement. So I left Donna, joined a health club where I worked off my gut and met muscular women, bought a rebuilt '68 Mustang, and started going to the Ginger Man.

Donna probably felt the same while married to me. Maybe, no, surely, she now feels the same as these women. And unlike me, like many of them, she is attracted to excitement but really wants habit and its comforts. So, like me, she is probably *seeing* a series of exciting men who, by their nature, maybe unknown to them, promise habit. We choose habit or excitement and risk breaking up our lives or our marriages if we try to balance them. Which is my point: none of us ever adds up to what we first seem or the promise we first inspire in a spouse or lover.

So you see, I know these women, I enjoy them, I love them, perhaps I cannot keep myself away from them. Maybe I cannot keep myself away from their dilemma. But there are difficulties in pursuing them, and lately, I suspect, problems with me.

I met Gena, of course, in the Ginger Man. She was old enough to have developed edges in her face, and those edges came together at the right angles, sloped in the right way, to make her face stunning. She was fighting a spreading butt with three-times-a-week aerobics and weight lifting, and the fight made her shine with health and fitness. Her hands moved with a smooth rhythm that resembled slow dancing. They glided up from her waist to her face as she talked.

She was talking to her friend Shan about Zen when I first saw her; seems Zen could help Shan with her growing disinterest in her husband. "Have you ever read Pirsig?" I asked.

Gena swivelled her head away from Shan and over to me. A smile spread across her face, and I noticed her dark eyebrows that made a canopy over her green eyes, giving her both a sensuous and a dangerous look. "I read the motorcycle thing when I was in college. Then I quit college and forgot about it."

Shan openly talked about her husband, who mostly ignored her. But Gena talked about touching and spirituality and lucky, rare times when, through sex, we could feel a partner's soul seeping through his or her own pores. How could I pass up an opportunity for rubbing metaphysical conceits, auras, souls, karma, with this attractive woman? So I left with her telephone number. However, we never made it into either one of our beds or received some mutual metaphysical massage.

Two weeks later, I drove to her house and went with her and her kids to see *Teenage Mutant Ninja Turtles Part III*. Since I had no kids of my own, the Turtle fad had escaped me. I sat in a dark theater, Gena next to me, from midway through the movie with my hand in hers and watched her seven-year-old boy and eleven-year-old girl stare up at the screen at fake turtles doing karate chops. Jason's mouth hung open, and he mimicked the moves of the turtles. Jennifer was too cool for participation. She slumped in her chair, cocked her head, feigned indifference, but she scooted up in her seat to watch the action scenes.

As I repeatedly checked my watch, I got a mixture of disgust, absurdity, and hopelessness because of the kids' interest and my intentions. But as I looked at Gena and her children, sometimes feeling Gena's hand tighten on mine as she too looked toward her children, her kids' reaction and her smile made *Teenage Mutant Ninja Turtles Part III* and my faint guilt tolerable. I would rather see the kids watch something with a semblance to reality, something like what I watched, cowboys and Indians, cops and robbers, spies and counter-spies, but even if vacuous, their reaction was amusing. And their amusement made their mother all the more desirable. She had done something; she had made these creatures whose uniqueness and charm I would discover if I stuck around. She had substance. And her substance came from the habit in her life, and here I was, Mr. Excitement.

Just before the climactic part of the picture, a crazy man stepped into the theater. I didn't see him, but I heard his low growl: "Gena." Once was not enough, "Gena, Gena, Gena Burleson." Gena's grip tightened on mine, and she hung her head. Jason quickly flipped himself backward, putting his knees in his seat, and looked over the back of his chair. Jennifer, like Mom, sunk into her seat. Jason uttered the word I feared, "Daddy."

"Maybe he'll go away," I whispered to Gena. "How can he know we're here?"

"No, no," Gena said. "He's convinced we're here. I know him. He'll stand there and scream until the movie's over." Gena stood up, I slumped down, and the moms, dads, and kids watching the *Teenage Mutant Ninja Turtles* shifted their eyes from the climactic fight to the lonely, disgusted, stunning woman walking up the theater aisle. She stopped in front of the man, and then they both stepped into the lobby.

I looked down the aisle. Jason just went back to watching the movie. Jennifer had her hands in front of her face. I scooted next to Jason. "What do you kids want to do?" I was depending upon a seven-year-old for advice.

Jason looked queerly at me. "Gee, I don't know, sir." Jennifer pulled her hands down, shot to her feet, scooted past me, and stormed up the aisle. The faces of the people in the audience again left the *Mutant Ninja turtles* to get a glimpse of one of the offspring of these insane people.

Jason swung his head between the back of the theater and the screen. I leaned over and whispered to him again, "Do you want to leave or watch the show?"

He cocked his head again, then whispered, "Let's go." I got up and stepped to one side as he scooted in front of me and walked up the aisle. As the Turtle fans again turned their attention to see the other offspring and the odd home-wrecker who started that disturbance, Jason grabbed my hand, maybe because he had no other adult's hand near him.

As Jason and I stepped from the dark theater into the lighted lobby, I heard, "Who is he?"

"I'm Don," I said, let go of Jason's hand, and offered my hand. The husband didn't speak; he stared at me, then turned to his wife. I lowered my hand and Jason grabbed it again.

"I just wasn't ready for this."

"You were the one who moved out," Gena said.

"I was just driving by the house. I noticed some souped-up Mustang."

"You promised not to ***just drive by***."

"I'm not taking this well." Gena's husband stepped back from her, then turned his attention to me. His brows wrinkled as if he were searching through his mind for some kind of clue. Some recall of scenes from movies or of locker room talk or some suppressed primordial memory must have flickered behind his eyes: "Just what the hell do you think you're doing?" Jason squeezed my hand.

"Kenneth," Gena shouted, "we're separated."

I needed to defend myself. "I took a lovely woman and her kids to the movie."

"I suppose you're proud of yourself?"

This small woman squared herself on her strong,

well-developed legs, prepared even to duke it out if necessary, and gave her rationale: "Kenneth, we've both ***seen*** other people." There was that word ***seen***. Kenneth and I both recognized it. In the lingo of the newly separated or divorced, ***seeing, to see***, or ***seen*** can mean dating, screwing or merely meeting for lunch. And because it could mean all these things, the word tormented Kenneth. And Gena, embarrassed and humiliated, meant to hurt him by using the word. These are the emotions aroused by disrupted habit.

Kenneth thought for a moment: "We didn't say anything about him." It was a desperate statement. I wanted to laugh or pat him on the shoulder. Gena looked away from him, as though he was now beyond all rational action, thought, or words.

"Leave us alone. Go away," Jennifer said to her father. Kenneth backed up, away from his family, and leaned against a movie poster for *Teenage Mutant Ninja Turtles Part III*.

Jason started to cry and squeezed my hand. Then he looked up to see whose hand he was squeezing, the weird man Mom had asked to the movies. This hand not being appropriate, he looked at his family, let go of my hand, and wrapped his arms around his mother.

"Look at this," she said, and a shiver, a silent sob, or just a great knot of tension, embarrassment, and disappointment shook Kenneth's shoulders. He looked away from us. Gena's voice softened, "Let's discuss this at home."

Kenneth glanced once at me before he turned and led his family outside of the theater, like a cowardly lion leading his pride away, Gena first, then Jennifer pulling Jason. I stepped closer to the exit door to watch Gena and the kids pile into her Suburban, and Kenneth follow them in his Buick. As I watched, the audience filed out of *Teenage Mutant Ninja Turtles III*, and like one giant creature with hundreds of eyes, the audience now stared harshly at me, the bold sleazy home-wrecker.

I suffered through the stares, walked out of the theater, called a taxi to take me home. Late that night, Gena called me, and I called a taxi to take me to her house to get my car. I walked up the dark driveway, thinking that I'd never see the bullet that got me. As I neared my car, a light came on, and Gena appeared from out of the garage. I jumped back, "Don, it's me," she said. "He's gone again, for now."

She walked up to me. Her hands rose effortlessly up from her side and then stretched out for me, and I hesitantly raised my arms and wrapped them around her. A wayward light caught in the angles of her face and darkened the indentations just under her cheek and brightened the prominent cheekbones. She looked up at me, and we kissed. It was a labored kiss of stifled passion, a kiss that made promises of erotic adventures and the possibility of real love. It felt like sex, like want, like regret, like hope. "I guess I won't see much of you," she said.

"Let's try it again," I said.

"Let's give it some time. Let's give Kenneth some time," she said and kissed me again. And I knew that she and Kenneth would both need a lot of time.

As I walked down the Burleson driveway, a driveway and a house that will probably soon be on the market, I heard the clichés that certain amateur psychologists say about me: I go out with married women to avoid commitment. But this cliché is at best one-third true. The other two-thirds is that these women retain a bit of themselves, their married lives, and I retain a bit of myself, my entire spectrum of women, my weekends, my nights out by myself or with the boys, so that we never completely ***have*** one another, so the unattainable mystery keeps the affair exciting and new. That's the key. They have habit. I left it behind. To them, I am different. So for a while, I can be exciting.

After Gena, I thought maybe I ought to try someone even less married than Gena. Chris was exuberantly young. While Gena was compact, Chris was lean and long, still young enough not to have to battle her body. She did not have the grace, the features of Gena, but she had that energy that the young have. While standing still, she almost seemed to bounce on her toes. Because she is tall, she loped into the Ginger Man and sat at the only seat available: the bar stool next to mine.

A week later, after the meal, the play, the drinks, she suggested that we drive to her parents' cabin, far north of Houston, past the northern suburbs and adjacent towns, way off into the piney woods, where we could hear the soft rain on the tin roof and be so completely alone.

On the way out, past the city limits, while we were cruising at seventy in my Mustang, Chris put her hand on my knee, "You know I have a boyfriend. Do you mind?"

"I didn't ask him out," I said.

"You're cool," she said and leaned across my console seat to kiss me.

"And you are wonderfully young," I said and kissed her.

Later, with her head resting on my arm, listening to a winter rain plop against the tin roof of her parents' cabin, Chris pushed her face into the hair on my chest. "You're cute," she said. I, of course, wanted to be more than cute. But I could appreciate Chris, not so much for specifically ***who*** she was, as I could appreciate Gena, but for ***what*** she was: a change of direction, a new course, a woman with no strings attached. She was more of the generic variety of woman.

Before I could answer with wit or compliments, a

fist banged on the door. "Just ignore it," I said.

A shout, "Chris, open up this goddamn door," accompanied the next bang.

"Oh my God," Chris said and looked at me, "It's Steve." She sprang to her feet. In the hazy light from the bathroom, I saw her taut body. Chris didn't have the curves and sags, and thus the character of Gena, but for just plain athletic appeal, she was fun to look at.

"Who's Steve?" I asked.

Before she could answer, before I could get dressed, Chris had jumped into her jeans and run out the bedroom door. When I heard the door creak open, I practically squinted my ears. I heard a man's voice. "So just what the hell do you think you're doing?"

"Chill, Steve," she said.

"Hi, Chris," a third voice said.

"Oh, hi, hi," Chris said.

"Who the goddamn hell is with you? You forget where you were supposed to be? You were going to goddamn meet me."

"Steve, you have a guest. Chill out."

Up until then, because of the thrill and romance of being where I was, some part of my mind suppressed my fear. I didn't know I was even scared until a thought formed in my gut and crawled up my throat and into my brain: there was no back door.

"So where is he?" Steve said again.

"Steve, maybe I ought to go," the third voice said.

"You're with me."

"Maybe we ought to go."

"And, I have a guest," Chris continued. "I'm here with a friend. He's in the bathroom," Chris said. My mind betrayed me; panic set in; I could not think. So I dressed, as fast as I could, scrambling to find underwear, socks, shoes, shirt. And just as I finished twisting myself into my clothes, just as I was about to reach for the bedroom door, I saw from the bathroom light, Chris's panties lying on the bed. I thought about chewing them and swallowing them. Instead, I stuffed them into one of my pockets and opened the bedroom door to accept my fate.

I saw Chris smiling; then I saw two zebras. Steve and his friend had on the black slacks and striped black and white shirts of basketball officials. One of the zebras cocked his head to stare at me. I stuck out my hand. "Steve," I said.

"No, Kenneth," the man said. My memory clicked back on, and I hoped that my face didn't show what I remembered: he was indeed Gena's husband. My reason kicked in, and I realized that it was not just possible but completely probable that I was going to be hurt.

The other zebra eyed me then turned to Chris: "Who the hell is he? Who the hell is he?"

"A friend," Chris said.

I reached into my back pocket, pulled out a card, and handed it to Steve. "Don," I said. "Chris tells me that her parents might be interested in selling this place."

"See. It's business," Chris said.

"Bullshit. Bullshit," Steve said, pushed Chris to one side and started for me. As I stepped back, thinking about covering up, Kenneth stepped in between us.

"Forget it, buddy," Kenneth said. "It's not worth it."

"The son of a . . ."

Kenneth didn't let him finish. "He's on the up and up. I've met him. He's a friend of my wife's."

Kenneth took me by the arm and led me toward the door.

"Chris, you can get a ride back, I guess," I said.

"Hurry," Kenneth whispered to me.

"Wait," Steve said as Kenneth opened the door. "He didn't even know you when he walked out here." He stepped toward us, but Chris wrapped her arms around him and kissed him.

Outside, on our way to the car, the rain running down our faces, I stopped and looked at Kenneth. "Why?"

"We referee basketball games together," Kenneth answered the wrong question. "We like to have a few drinks afterward. Steve wanted me to meet his new girlfriend. She wasn't at the bar, so we came here."

"No, no. Not that. Why did you help me?"

Kenneth now answered the right question: "I don't want to see Steve hurt. He's a married man."

"Thanks," I said. "How's your marriage?"

"God damn. You are a cruel son of a bitch."

"No, no. I mean it. I didn't have time but for one date, but I like Gena. How's your marriage?"

"We're still separated." He turned away from me, stopped, then turned back to face me, "What is it to you?"

"Nothing," I said, backing toward my car.

"You hanging around my wife? You gonna leave here and go back to my house?"

"No," I said.

He stopped walking toward me, hung his head, then looked up at me, "I'm a little touchy. But Steve's a lot more touchy. And I still don't trust you. Get your ass outta here."

I got in my Mustang and sprayed mud, hopefully not on Kenneth, and drove out of what I had thought was a dark safe haven. As I pulled back into Houston and city street lamps, I remembered Chris's panties in my pocket. I pulled them out and then noticed that I had my shirt on inside out.

In following my fascination with these women, I always knew that husbands were dangerous for me, but I figured out that I am also dangerous for husbands. Steve didn't seem to matter; he seemed too brutish. But I had hurt Kenneth; I didn't regret what I did – Gena was worth it – but I was sorry that he had to suffer. Kenneth saw that I was pushing for something that no doubt already eluded his grasp, his charm, his total capacity to ever retrieve. I came close to violating something that was ***his***. I do not say ***his*** to be condescending. Most assuredly, I was tampering with something that truly was his. She had, in whatever she was to him, become so much a part of what he considered himself to be that I, in taking a part of what he was to himself out to see *Teenage Mutant Ninja Turtles Part III*, was stealing something of ***him*** away from him. And I think that when he covered for me with Steve, he realized that, with or without me, he had already lost what he wanted. Habit and love make us like Kenneth. Steve was just jealous.

Needless to say, I got a bit concerned for my health. Disease is not the only risk in sex. I'm not really superstitious or a believer in fate, but two incidents, so close together, showed me that I was pushing my luck or that some kind of faulty wiring in my psyche or some overactive hormones were making my life precarious. I started sitting off by myself in the Ginger Man, in a corner where no women could come near me. I sipped my drinks and thought that what I now wanted, once again, was habit, the chance to feel as strongly about one woman as Kenneth Burleson. But I was scared of excitement. And as Donna, Gena, Kenneth, and all of us know, you have to risk excitement to find someone to start your habits.

The therapist I started going to first told me that I was afraid of commitment, then that I had some unfinished psychological accounts to settle with my mother, and when those two explanations seemed to have no effect on me, that I was addicted to sexual excitement. I knew all of this or could have guessed it or read it for myself. What my therapist left out was my genuine appreciation for everything that certain women can be. What my therapist does not say is that I am scared of wanting what I can't have. I should cancel my appointments, but when my therapist listens to my stories and tells me what to do, when her knees slip out from under her skirt and her perfume fills her office, I tell myself that this could be the start of something habit-forming. ■

BOOMTIMES

June 10, 1981

My phone bill is going to have three very large digits. Russ is going to shit green Twinkies when he gets it. I have called everybody back in Houston. Sometimes, I call my mother twice a day. Still, calling does not fill the whole day, so when I don't call, I write this. It is my book. Well, it is not really a book but a word processor file. I call it *my book* because it is just that, mine alone, for me only; no one else will ever read it.

I am beginning to feel like those pioneer women who moved out on the prairie and recorded their insanity and depression in journals and diaries. I now understand how, left at home, a woman is tempted to strip off her clothes and run naked into the open wilderness. Being a housewife – *oh, God, a housewife is really what I am* – in this barren, windswept place either dangerously numbs or excites your mind.

Jesus, I miss Houston. I remember the sour smelling drainage ditch behind our house that became just like one of the bayous when it rained. I used to be so bitchy about the humidity, the way it destroyed any way I fixed my hair and made me sweat through my makeup. Houston had nearly foot-long mosquitoes. Now, I'd kiss a mosquito's stinger and bathe in a drainage ditch. I'd settle for Russ getting transferred to Lafayette or some other rotten Louisiana town to get out of this bone-dry heat and back to civilization. I used to mock those rigid middle-class women with Montgomery Ward charge cards, but now I want to walk in a mall and drive on a freeway.

Sometimes, in the late afternoons, I drive to the end of Fort Stockton and get on IH-10, look down that arrow-straight road, and pretend I can see Houston at the other end of it. It hasn't rained once in the three months we've been here. In Houston, I'd be complaining about the rain. Dust blows in through the caulking around the windows. In sunbeams, I can see not only motes but layers of dust floating down through the air onto my furniture. Sometimes I remember even further back beyond Houston to college. It would be fantastically wonderful to be back in college and dating Russ, living with Debi Hurt, and reading books that pass for real literature.

Worse, I live in a terrible house. This oil boom mess has driven up the prices of homes even here in Fort Stockton. I hear it is even worse in Midland. And with all the geologists, other accountants, district executives, inspectors, and such moving in with their families, we were lucky to find a house. We had to take what we could get. And since Russ is not sure how long he will be here (he first supposed just long enough to fix the books up for the Exxon people), he thought we should buy as cheap as possible. So, we bought a nicely arranged but small two-bedroom. I've done quite well with the inside of my house: good beige carpet, white drapes in front, Levolor blinds on the other windows, a ceiling fan, and my wedding-present furniture. The exterior, though, is the pits. No one in

Fort Stockton cares a damn about beautification. They just bulldoze and build: no trees, no lawns, no parks. Our front yard was hard-packed caliche. I paid a dear price for a lawn and continue to pay dearly to water it. So I have some green around our house. But beyond my front yard is nothing but desert. For the first few weeks, I kept my blinds and my drapes closed, sat in my dark house, read, and waited for Russ to come home for a dinner, some talk, some TV, and sex. But after a while, I started pulling open the drapes to my front window to watch my neighbors.

We are not in the best part of town, if Fort Dullsville even has a nice part of town. We live next door to a charming Hispanic family.

Their front yard is still hard-packed dirt, as mine was. When the wind blows, which is mostly always, their dirt blows in through my front windows. I told the poor lady – girl, really – that if she just squirted some water on the dirt it wouldn't blow so much. She does so regularly now, and smiles and nods at me and says *bueno*, then shakes her head, and says "nice." She is cute when she smiles at me and tries to speak English. She has small hips and large breasts but still looks too much like a girl to be a mother. When she waters her dirt and makes puddles and tiny, shallow lakes in her front yard, her little girl runs out of the house, sheds all of her clothes, squats in the mud puddles. That darling baby rubs it into her nose, mouth, eyes, and hair. I want to pull her out of the mud and bathe her. But the Hispanic lady just sits on the steps of her porch and laughs, and the little girl splashes in the mud.

Neither mother nor daughter ever wears shoes. At the end of the day, both have dirt caked to their calves and ankles from squatting and playing in the bare front yard. The precious little baby girl starts the day in a T-shirt and shorts. But by mid-afternoon, she stomps through the dirt, bare-chested in dirty Pampers. And about 4:30, she and her mother sit in the swing on their front porch, her one possession that I envy her for, dangle their dirty legs over its edge, sing in Spanish, and wait for the coarse-looking husband. When her husband comes home in his dirty, greasy oil-field clothes, the lady/girl/mother leaps off the swing, leaving the little girl giggling in the rapidly swaying swing, runs to him, jumps, and wraps her dirty legs around him while he cradles her behind with one arm. And, pressing against her sweaty, greasy, smelly husband, she spreads her wide lips around his thin ones, sucking at his mouth rather than kissing. Russ once got home the same time as her husband, and poor, shy Russ waved to the young man, but then ducked his head, pretending not to notice, as the young, little wife jumped into him.

I haven't turned into a bigot since I have been here, but these people are just different. They have their charm, especially the little girl. Russ, the capitalist accountant, has made me less idealistic. He tells me that it is all economic. The poor people just don't have the money to lift themselves to any sort of privilege or self-awareness. He says he knows as well as I that people are conditioned by socio-economic conditions but that we must accept inequalities because they are inevitable. We can only try our best not to hurt other people and try to stop them from hurting themselves. A stronger social structure may give them far more potential for advancement than any reforms. I sometimes agree with him now. I even voted Republican in the last election. In college, I felt that voting Republican was something that we used to consider dirty, like oral sex, but just had to try. But now, living with Russ and associating with his people, stuck in West Texas, I may start campaigning for Republican candidates.

Russ tells me, when he gets home and gently kisses me then reads his newspaper, to pay no attention to the neighbors, not to watch them. But before dinner, I always take a last glance out my front window at the hugging, obscenely kissing couple and the swinging little girl. They are somehow different from us.

June 22, 1981

Her name is Elodia Ramírez, and she calls her husband Frankie. Because I stay home most of the day, though I've looked for a job but would just as soon not fry hamburgers or type for some chauvinist in a cowboy hat and pointy-toe boots, I introduced myself to her. She bowed her head when I told her my name, and her child wrapped her little arms around her mother's knees. Elodia bent and pulled the little girl up to her chest as though showing me a trophy. The little girl, then the mother, smiled, and I reached to the little girl to wipe some of the dried mud from her cheek. Hefting the child, Elodia said, "Betty." Hispanics try to Americanize themselves so much with the names of their children, but they always seem to choose outdated, old-fashioned names. I expect to someday see a little Hispanic girl named Clara, like my grandmother.

I invited her over for a cup of coffee, and she looked down again. Betty wriggled down from Elodia's chest, and I picked her up. She bowed her head too and looked back at her mother. "Please," I said, and Elodia agreed to come over. First, though, she grabbed her daughter from me, ran into her house, and came out with a pair of low-heeled pumps on her bare feet. I wanted to laugh at her, but, in a secret way, I was glad they would not tromp mud and dirt through my living room.

Elodia waited in the frame of my living room door until I signaled for her to come in. Her head swiveled on her neck as she looked at my furniture; then she looked at my rather expressionistic painting, the one that my girlfriend Debi did of Russ, and said, "Pretty." In college, Debi and I used to talk so much trash about people who called art ***pretty***. She held her daughter's hand and pulled her closer to the painting and twisted her head to look at the painting. In college, Joey Fowler, an obnoxious Lambda Chi from the piney woods, would always say that his dumb friend reading algebra looked like a hog looking at a watch. Elodia knew as much about what to see in the painting as Joey Fowler's hog. But ***pretty*** was a compliment from a woman who knew little about art or English.

I told her to sit down, and she and her daughter sat down on my sofa. The little girl tried to get up, but Elodia pulled her back down beside her, making the little girl whimper. "Oh, let her loose," I told Elodia, but the mother insisted that the little girl stay right beside her. I got Elodia and myself cups of coffee and got Betty a soda. Betty drank while we sipped, and I found out that Frankie was an American, born in Presidio, which from what I have heard, is a God-awful hellhole worse than Fort Stockton. She married him just after she and her parents had moved to Ojinaga, the border town across the border from Presidio, from Chihuahua City. Nobody makes money in Presidio. But any money is better than what either Frankie or Elodia could make in Ojinaga, so they first lived in Presidio, then moved farther north so Frankie could work in the oil fields and Elodia could learn English.

When she left, I felt like Scarlett O'Hara, or maybe Lady Bird Johnson, or some crotchety, rich Texas matriarch who thought herself liberated because she condescended to talk to some darky or a Mexican. Elodia just absolutely reeked with subservience. Like the stereotypes, like the Hollywood Hispanics in Western movies, she lowered her eyes, whispered to me, talked only when I asked a direct question.

That night, just as we went to bed, Russ already snoring, too tired that night for much nastiness, I heard a faint scream from the shy, head-dropping Elodia. I got up from bed and ran into the living room so I could hear better. Then I heard her scream again and knew it was the low then high-pitched ascending scream a woman lets go just before she has the big O.

The next morning, I asked her back for coffee. She was reluctant to talk to me, but I asked her more questions, thus forcing some more conversation out of her. At our third coffee klatch, she asked me about Russ in stuttering, hesitant English. At our next coffee, she allowed the little girl to bring some toys over and play between us, Elodia on the sofa and I on the recliner. She loosened up, and we talked like giggly coeds. Tee hee.

On a later visit, after she had gotten used to me and told me about herself, in what English she had, I noticed a bit of sweat form on her chest and stomach so that her baggy white blouse stuck to the top roll in her tummy. I could see that she was pregnant. Russ and I had been trying for two years. Why am I so screwy?

July 7, 1981

I joined the Junior League! Mother is not yet tired of my calls. I've read most of what interests me at the one bookstore in town, **Walden's**, and I've seen all of this month's movies and specials on HBO. I had friends in Houston, and restaurants where we used to sip good coffee all morning and watch the drizzle, and all the parks with their trees, and, Jesus, the bars. I want to dance to rock-and-roll again and hear some jazz. The closest thing here is the League.

Russ suggested I join after the people he worked with asked about me. I went in ready to say the F word in front of the dainty Leaguers, but I found that I could actually like most of them. The Junior League is kind of a cosmopolitan bunch here in Fort Stockton. Hardly any of us are from West Texas, and those who are have been away long enough that we talk about something other than the Baptist Church or drinking beer. We even tell League jokes: *Why don't Junior Leaguers go to orgies? Too many thank-you notes.*

July 19, 1981

I'm pregnant! I have this feeling that writing it down, p-r-e-g-n-a-n-t, makes it more official. To celebrate, Russ joined the country club, or what Fort Stockton calls a country club. I got a little bitchy with him, because I was still not used to admitting that I was now a Junior Leaguer. But last night, we went to eat at the *club* and I was all set to dislike the unsophisticated mid-rich who had pretensions toward looking rich. But wowie kazowie, again I met some of the people Russ works with and I liked them. Most are fairly young and, oh, boy, just starting families. They really seemed to have no pretensions at all.

Yesterday, I went to the pool and met Lois, the wife of the loan officer at one of the bigger banks in town, and Jill, the wife of Fort Stockton's newest pediatrician and the man who will now take care of my child, and Jordon, the wife of a rancher who found oil on his property. Lois is the bitchiest of the three, but she is amusing. She told me another Junior League joke. *How does a girl get kicked out of the league? She sells the Suburban, gets a job, or has an orgasm.* These are not the people I thought I'd like, especially back in college. But these women all seem to have been to college or have yearned for a liberal-artsy education; we all seem to be potential Peace Corps volunteers, social workers, or high school English teachers; but we all seem to have married well; that is, we all seem to have married financially able men, the type of men we were always taught we should marry but swore we never would.

When I did what most pregnant, country-clubbing Junior Leaguers do, shop for maternity wear and baby clothes, although the selection is kind of limited in Fort Stockton, mostly T-shirts with big red arrows pointing to your belly and the word ***BABY***, I also bought a blouse for Elodia. She was ahead of me and getting more rounded, so she had started wearing Frankie's T-shirts. I gave her a maternity blouse with pockets low in the front so the preggy could reach into her shirt and feel her baby. Elodia smiled, then dropped her head. Her bowed head must have pissed me off. I stuck my hand under her chin and lifted it back up so that I could see her eyes. I forced myself to smile, but her smile dropped into a frown, and she took a step back from me. I invited her in for coffee or a Coke. Before she could accept my offer, her little girl ran out of her house, leaving the screen door bouncing behind her, and told her mother to come quickly to watch something on TV. Elodia smiled at me and shrugged her shoulders.

Strangely, the next day, early, before ten, Elodia rang my door bell and gave the blouse back. She said that Frankie ordered her to give the shirt back. He had said that she didn't need it and that he didn't want the *gringa's* shirt. They were not *pelados*. The racist bastard. That is stupid, to reject something given out of affection, something really needed, out of some misplaced pride. Her little girl yelled for her, "Momma, Momma," and Elodia smiled at me and bowed her head. Then, as if she had understood what I had tried to say the day before, she lifted her head and smiled at me. I patted her shoulder and asked her to reconsider the blouse. She kept her smile on her face but shook her head; then daintily, gracefully, like a sprite or a child, she skipped across my front yard and into hers to hurry to Betty.

A night or so later, after Elodia gave the blouse back, a low scream woke me up. Russ was curled away from me and snoring. I poked him, but he didn't wake up. I heard a low growl that turned into a shriek, and I remembered it as Elodia's orgasmic scream. So I tiptoed, as though she could have heard me, from our bedroom and into the living room. I pulled at the sides of one of my front drapes and squinted to look at the Ramirez house. And, after my eyes adjusted, I could see Frankie and Elodia naked, their skin silvery and shining in the bright moonlight, sitting in their front porch swing. I squinted to see Frankie sitting in the swing, pushing it gently back and forth with the balls of his naked feet and Elodia, turned in to face him, squatting on his lap, with her legs wrapped around his waist. She leaned back, and he held on to her elbows to keep her from falling over backwards. They bounced and swung as they screwed, and her slightly swollen pregnant belly bumped against his slightly swollen beer belly.

Russ was going to have to see this. I ran back into the bedroom and shook him until he woke up. He reached for his glasses on the night stand and put them on to glare at me. I held my finger to my lip and told him that he had to come look. I pulled him out of bed and into the living room, and he got to the window just in time to hear one of Elodia's growls and to see a couple more swings and bounces. Then, as Russ and I, our cheeks pressed together so we could both see out the window, watched, they both shivered then went limp in a simultaneous orgasm.

Russ pulled the drape back and sat down on the sofa. I peeked out again. "Leave them to their own business," Russ said to me.

I turned around to him. "How can you not watch?" I turned to peek out again.

He told me that he thought what they were doing was ***disgusting***. I told him not to be such an old Puritan. But sitting in the dark in his pajamas with his thick glasses sitting lopsided on the bridge of his nose, he looked like an old Puritan. "I'm not a Puritan," he said. "But even hormonal fraternity boys have more modesty and sense of propriety," he said.

Propriety! Until then, I couldn't imagine anyone my age using that word. He wanted to go back to bed and leave them to their privacy. He didn't want to watch. He wasn't even curious. Then he said, "Aren't you being just a little perverse here?" God, two people were fucking their brains out right in front of our window, and Russ wasn't even interested. "It's sick," he said. I thought it was exciting, sensual, romantic, and I told him so and snuck another look. Then he said, "Come to bed."

"Let's do it now," I pleaded.

"Let's just go to bed." Russ stood up and took his glasses off.

"Didn't you get excited?"

"My God, the crazy woman is pregnant."

"So what does that mean?"

"It means that she's pregnant and should watch herself."

"You're kidding."

"Let's go to bed." Russ turned and walked to the bedroom.

We didn't screw that night.

August 5, 1981

Russ and I have had no sex since. He looks at me lying on my back some nights as I rub my stomach and try to feel our child, then rolls away from me and goes to sleep. I stay awake listening to his snores. This morning, sleepy, I write this down. I cannot write in this book, I can't even boot it up, when Russ is in the house.

I've wanted to call my friends in Houston late at night to tell them how scared I've suddenly become. But I can't bring myself to make the call.

I have tried to ask the ***girls*** at the country club for advice. Jordon, who is a great deal younger than her husband, says that Decker, her old husband, can no longer perform every night either. Lois was quick to point out that Russ was still a young man, "a stud," she said. Jordon, an ex--Chi Omega from Baylor, got a bit irritated and said that Decker could keep up with any man she ever had. Lois, growing a bit bitchy and unable to resist cattiness, said, "And how much experience could you have had, dating Baptist frat boys and old men?" We all laughed at each other, my question effectively ignored and Jordon a little pissed. Later, Jill, the oldest, told me that I have no real problem at all. She explained that some men who see their wives pregnant a first time are shocked. I've just barely started to show, and I told Jill. Still, she told me, the idea just turns some men's hormones mushy.

I am growing more and more like the women at the club and in the League who grow more and more dependent upon an important man in town. There is a desperation at these meetings, *a quiet desperation* Thoreau might say. A couple of times, while at the country club pool, I tried to imagine Elodia there with me. I could imagine her going gaga-eyed over the trimmed golf course and the clean pool. Usually, after imagining her there, I feel terribly guilty for conjuring up an embarrassment for her.

So I am skipping a couple of days at the country club to watch and entertain Elodia. I invite her in and we talk about babies. Our conversations are not the witty, silly, or bitchy talks I have with Lois, Jill, and Jordon, but I am beginning to enjoy her company more and more and to trust her judgment. She looks at me now and talks in a normal manner that doesn't make her seem a peon. In a way, I am proud of her. I begin to wonder if I should admit my problem – hell, Russ's problem – to this poor, simple, pregnant woman who screws while sitting backwards in a swing.

To keep from thinking about Russ, I dote on my baby. My belly is growing more rounded now, and I lie naked in my bed at night and feel it as though it were a rising loaf of bread. One night, Russ woke up in the dark and rolled toward me to see me rubbing my belly. "Honey," he whispered. I rolled to him and kissed him and wrapped my one leg over his thigh. He kissed back but gently pulled away from me. I asked him what was wrong.

"Nothing," he said and rolled away from me. I reached around him and asked him to at least hold me. He held on to my arm, squeezed it slightly, and said, "We just shouldn't be fooling around much while you're pregnant."

"Who told you that?" I asked.

"We just shouldn't," he said.

"What about Elodia and Frankie?"

"Well, just look at them," he said. I kept silent. And since then, I remain silent during the nights. Sometimes I go to bed after Russ is already asleep. I wake late. Some nights I cannot sleep, so I write this down. Some nights, I listen for ultra-pregnant Elodia screaming out her orgasms.

August 24, 1981

Two nights ago, while I was watching *Cagney & Lacy* and Russ was doing some work that he had brought home, I heard Elodia scream, not her sexual scream but one that was sustained and purposeful. I got up and opened the door. But before I could take another step out of the door, Russ had come up behind me, grabbed me, and told me not to go over to her house.

And I remember very distinctly that I said, "Let me go, goddamn it." Russ did let go, but I didn't run toward Elodia's house. I turned to look at Russ. He was shocked and, as Elodia had done, hung his head. "Don't go over there," he said. Elodia screamed in Spanish. I stepped off the front porch, and Russ came up behind and put his arms around me, not to hold me back but to hug me. "Please don't go over there. It is their business."

We both saw a light go on; then, the shadow of Frankie, stretching large and tall because of the dim light, pushed the shadow of Elodia. We heard her scream again. Russ turned toward our house and dragged me after him. I tugged once against his arm, then let him pull me because I knew that I was really too scared to run to their house. Russ called the police, and we sat on the front porch listening to Elodia and Frankie scream at each other. Then we heard things crashing and breaking.

When the police pulled up in two different cars, Russ stood up and pointed toward the Ramírez house. Two policemen went to the Ramírez's door, and a third, who had pulled up by himself, stayed with us. Russ, the policeman, and I slowly crept across the front lawn. When a gun went off, the policeman pushed Russ and me flat into our lawn, and the two policemen at the door pulled their guns and kicked the Ramírez's door down. In several minutes, the two policemen came out with Frankie handcuffed. Elodia came out behind the policemen. Russ, the policeman with us, and I stood up. A chill that the cooling grass gave me made me shake. Then, seeing Frankie look at me made me shiver. He had blood on his face, but it was not his own blood. Elodia blinked against blood that seeped from a cut across her forehead. She ran up behind one of the policemen who guided Frankie and hit him square between the shoulders with a back-handed fist. Betty, the poor little daughter, came to the open door and stared at her parents. Frankie dug his heels into his lawn, and the police tugged on his arms. Elodia grabbed his waist and pulled him from behind.

I could see that she was crying. Frankie, looking over his shoulder, was crying, too. Poor Betty started crying. The policeman with Russ and me ran from us and grabbed Elodia. Frankie tried to jerk away when he saw the policeman grab his wife, and one of the policemen holding him let go of him with one hand, grabbed his nightstick with the other, and split Frankie's head open.

While Elodia sobbed and wiggled within the policeman's arms and as little Betty ran to her mother, the other two policemen threw Frankie into the back seat of their car. When they drove off, the policeman with Elodia guided her back toward the house and pulled a handkerchief out of his pocket to dab at the blood on her forehead. As Elodia stepped up the stairs of her porch, she pushed against the policeman and pulled herself and her daughter to the large swing. The policeman let her sit down. He then ran for his car to call an ambulance.

I left Russ and started to run to Elodia. As I got closer, she pulled her head up from her child to glare at me. She knew that Russ and I had called the cops. I stopped in my tracks. Russ came back up beside me and whispered in my ear for me to go back to our house.

Elodia was back home from the hospital before Russ left for work. I called the police station and found out that Frankie was drunk and for some reason had started the fight. Elodia had picked up a knife, but Frankie had gotten it away from her and sliced her forehead. He knocked her down, and she ran to her bedroom and came back with the pistol that they keep in the closet. She shot at him but missed.

With some more calls, I found out that Frankie was in jail for wife abuse and suspected for some other hazy crimes. Little Betty was in a children's welfare home until a trial. I found out that Frankie could do time and Elodia could lose Betty. At noon, Russ called and told me that he had demanded a transfer. The division chief promised that in six months we'd both be out of Ft. Stockton. In the meantime, Russ promised, we'd be out of our present house.

By early afternoon, Elodia had come out of her house. She sat in her front porch swing and gently rocked back and forth. She held her swollen, pregnant belly as if she were hurting. I couldn't just spy. I had to say something. So I stepped out of my house, took a deep breath, and walked across my yard to Elodia. "Dear, dear Elodia," I said, "if there is anything that I can possibly do . . . ."

Elodia held her stomach and rose up out of the swing. She looked me squarely in the eye and yelled, ***"Puta, puta, puta,"*** at me. I stood where I was for as long as I could, but finally I turned and ran back toward my house. Elodia ran after me and screamed, ***"Puta, puta, puta."*** I closed my door behind me, but Elodia stepped up on my porch and whined like a cat in heat, ***"Puta, puta, puta."***

They are gone now; they moved before we did. I stayed at the front door and watched as friends loaded their furniture onto a pickup. I didn't dare step out. I told Russ that they had moved, and he said, "Thank God," and he hugged me. To celebrate, we ate at the country club. Jill was there with her husband, my pediatrician. She hugged me, said she had heard, and promised to help look for a new house for us. Her husband patted my belly and said both the baby and I were doing just fine.

Now I am at home. Russ is in bed, probably already asleep. I can write now with him in the house. I don't even care if he calls up the file that this is on. I sit in my dark living room and stare out of my drapes at the empty house next to mine. Then I remember, go to my computer, and write, as though the words can take what has happened to me and the way I feel away from me and transfer it all to my book.

Russ and I haven't made love, and now I don't want to. I try to sleep, but I keep hearing Elodia's different screams. The ***puta, puta, puta*** turns into her deep frightened scream that rose from her lungs when Frankie cut her and then that scream becomes her low sexual groan.

They are different from us. We should live in our own parts of town and be separate. All that gushy talk in college about equality and rights is fine in theory but wrong. We have to protect ourselves from them -- not because they themselves can hurt us but because they can make us hurt ourselves. I don't think that I want to be married to Russ anymore. I don't think I want my baby. ■

OCOTILLO

Some said Sister Quinn could turn into an owl, just like the souls of the dead, and perch during the night on the back country tombstones. Sister Quinn knew what some people said, and as she sat in the cold cab of Gilbert Mendoza's truck and stared into the dark, cold desert, she wished she could turn into an owl.

A beam of light then came across the desert and lit the withered arms of the ocotillos in gray shades and stopped Sister Quinn's wishing. The beam went out and left the ocotillo, creosote, lechuguilla, and quayacán as dark shapes shaking in the wind against a darker sky. Sister Quinn flashed the headlights of Gilbert Mendoza's pickup truck and again looked at the arms of the cacti in that beam of light. The way they shook and writhed in the wind, these desert plants could be showing their torment and rage, or they could be filled, like owls perched on tombstones, with the angry spirits of the dead.

Sister Quinn saw some *pelados* picking their way carefully through the rough desert between the Río Grande and the south rim. Cactus needles and mesquite thorns could work through the thin cloth of jeans, shirts, and tennis shoes and into human skin. A misdirected step into a lechuguilla would give a shiver of pain that would last several days. This time of year the rattlesnakes and scorpions were mostly burrowed in, but a stray might crawl out. A rock could turn and twist an ankle. All that Sister Quinn could do or maybe *would* do was to drive them to Presidio, past the border Patrol's check point, where a *coyote*, not a *simpático*, would drive them to El Paso. She blinked the headlights again to give the stumbling, fragile peasants a bearing.

Sister Quinn saw the leader of this ragged line hold his Levi's jacket closed with the fist of his left hand. Then, the desert lit up. The *probecitos* froze in the beams of light just like deer. The lights made two eerie worlds, one light, one dark. The lit world was black and white, but bright enough for Sister Quinn to see the dirty, sweat-stained jackets of the people, the vapor of their breath, and the near-green of the withered ocotillo arms that writhed in the wind.

Sister Quinn opened the door of Gilbert Mendoza's truck and stepped out into the dark, the cold, and the wind. Gilbert Mendoza was not a devout man, but he worried about her, so he lent her his truck, and he sent his youngest child, Azul, to help her with the upkeep of her chapel.

The wind hit her, and a shiver ran from her butt to her shoulders. She shook her shoulders and felt her large breasts and stomach jiggle. "Don't move," Sister Quinn heard and stood perfectly still. Then she heard an engine and tires biting into sand and rock. She heard more squealing tires. Policemen were chasing the *coyote* from Ojinaga who had dropped these people off in the middle of the nighttime Texas desert.

She looked toward the source of the light beams and made out the shape of a Border Patrol's four-wheel drive truck. She rotated, knowing that the Border Patrol would not shoot her, and ran, as fast as she could with her weight, toward the huddled-up *pilados*, who were paralyzed by the cold wind and head lights. Running, she saw Border Patrol agent Pat Coomer walking toward the group with a rifle cradled in his arm. She stopped. "When you going to stop this?" Then Coomer added, "Huh, *curandera*?"

Pat Coomer didn't believe or understand. Because Lupé Rodríguez had a lot of faith, Sister Quinn had positioned the old woman spread-eagled on a clean white sheet, put candles stuck in little glasses with the Virgin painted on them in each corner of the sheet, and prayed. The praying pulled the spirit that made Lupé sick out of her body and onto the sheet. The candles kept the spirit confined to the sheet. Then Sister Quinn burned the sheet to destroy the spirit. Sister Quinn didn't cure Lupé Rodríguez's cancer, but Lupé felt better while she waited to die and hadn't spent the money she needed for medicine on the *curanderos* in Ojinaga. And for her help, God had once allowed Sister Quinn to dream that she had turned into an owl and had perched all night on Lupé Rodríguez's tombstone.

Border Patrol agent Adolf Martínez walked up to Pat Coomer, and when Coomer raised his hand up, palm flat, Martínez hesitantly slapped it. "Did it, *Vato*," Coomer said. Dolph stared at Sister Quinn, and his face asked the same question that he always asked her: Why did she do this?

Four years before, way up, on a high trail above the rim, Sister Quinn found Agent Martínez trying to press his guts back into his body. A college boy with a back pack full of dope had shot him three times in the stomach. Sister Quinn did just what she would have done for any poor dying soul: gave him a vial with a silver-blue metallic liquid, the kind you could buy in

Ojinaga, and told him to pray. And as he clutched the vial against his bleeding stomach and tried to pray, Sister Quinn dragged him down and out of the dead zone and then used his walkie talkie to call for help.

The locals along Texas Highway 170, the old El Camino Real, weren't surprised. She was magical, they said. She always showed up when someone needed help. They called her a saint or a *buena curandera.* Sister Quinn was probably flying overhead, returning from her perch on a tombstone, they said, when she saw Dolph dying.

When Dolph Martínez gained enough consciousness to thank her and to hear her tell all about what had happened, he threw the glass vial at her and said, "Take back your voodoo shit."

"The cure doesn't matter," Sister Quinn said. "Only your strength and your belief. You don't need to believe in that potion."

"I don't."

"But you must believe in something."

Now, Martínez grabbed her arm and whispered, "Don't go closer." Sister Quinn watched as a half-circle of agents coralled the aliens. Sister Quinn pulled away from Dolph and started to run, as best as she could, toward them. "Hold on, Sister. Stop," she heard agent Pat Coomer say.

Before she could get much farther, Coomer was even with her and grabbed the fleshy back of her biceps. She looked up at Coomer and saw the lines that the Chihuahua desert sun burned into his once boyish face. "The first time didn't take, huh?" Coomer said, then quickly looked toward the group gathered in the headlight beams.

"*Arriba las Manos*," Sister Quinn heard like a litany. The chorus of Border Patrol Agents appeared from behind the dark shapes of boulders, mesquite, and creosote, and smaller beams of light, flashlight beams, appeared from each policeman and settled on the faces of the people with the raised hands. The peasants raised their hands slowly, looking around at each other, as though trying to get a cue from somebody as to what to do, as though looking for a leader.

"*Tira las pistolas*," Pat Coomer yelled.

"Good work, good work," Martínez whispered to Coomer as he stepped up beside Pat and Sister Quinn.

"These people have done nothing but been born on the wrong side of an artificial line," Sister Quinn yelled to Dolph.

"Shut up," Martínez yelled back at her. "My people need to hear my orders." Pat Coomer left her alone with Dolph and walked into the group and pushed them farther apart from one another.

"Let us go, Dolph," Sister Quinn said in a whisper. "Or keep me and let them go on."

"Can't you see?" Dolph said and pointed his flashlight beam toward the group. Pat Coomer opened one of the *moldado's* jacket, then pulled the front of his shirt open. A green plastic bag was taped to his belly. The man cringed when Pat Coomer ripped the bag off of his stomach and held it up toward Martínez.

Then, one of the Patrol agents started to scream, "A gun, one's got a gun."

Flashlights went out. The spotlight from a truck went out. And just as Dolph Martínez pushed her down, Sister Quinn saw agents jumping. Sister Quinn rolled and looked up to see Martínez's shining flashlight make a beam from each *mojado* straight back to him, making him an easy target. And then she saw Pat Coomer beside him holding a raised rifle. "Get down," Sister Quinn yelled to Dolph and Pat.

Dolph yelled, "There." And Pat Coomer levelled his rifle.

"*Para, Para*," Pat and Dolph yelled.

"What else can I do?" Pat whispered. "Give me an

order."

"Go on," Dolph said, "Shoot."

"And just as Pat fired, Sister Quinn jumped up, but Dolph Martínez got his foot in between hers and knocked her backwards. Pat's rifle thudded as Sister Quinn hit the ground.

"I think I got a piece of him," Pat Coomer said.

The flashlight beams came back and then the beam from a truck's spotlight.

Dolph knelt beside Sister Quinn. "Are you all right?"

"You're fascists," Sister said to Dolph and Pat.

"And you're a nun," Pat Coomer said. "Shame, shame, shame."

"These are just poor people."

"Jesus," Pat said, "when you going to stop that kind of preaching, *curandera*?"

"Because I minister to the people, because I give them faith and aid their faith, you call me a *curandera*. Greasewood tea can cure constipation. Doctors and scientists now say what the locals and Indians have known for centuries: *aloe vera* can cure nearly anything."

She stopped when she felt Dolph's grip on the fleshy part of her arm. "Shut up," he said quietly.

"You, You . . . ," Sister Quinn stumbled trying to call Pat Coomer something. "These are people, not animals to hunt."

"The son of a bitch shoulda known better," Pat said to her.

"Good shot," Dolph said. "He'll be easy enough to find in the morning. My recommendation is that we don't want to go stumbling around in the dark. Somebody'd fall off a cliff, get stung or bit. Better to wait until daylight."

Sister Quinn said, "I'll look for him if you're too scared to. You owe it to him now that you shot him."

Dolph said, "Bring her to the car and read her her rights." He walked toward the parked trucks.

Pat Coomer grabbed her biceps and tried to pull her up, but Sister Quinn planted her feet and her girth into the loose desert rock. "God damn it. Nun or not, get your ass moving," Coomer said.

"We've got to go after him," Sister Quinn said.

"Don't make me use cuffs this time," Coomer said. "That man ran...."

"Because he was scared," Sister Quinn interrupted.

"He ran because he was carrying dope," Coomer said. "Somebody on one side of the border or the other will eventually kill him."

Sister Quinn grunted and pulled her arm out of Coomer's grip. "He was a Salvadoran refugee. That is why he ran. That is why I am here to pick him up. You shot a political refugee."

Before she knew what was happening, Sister Quinn's feet were out from under her and Pat Coomer grunted as he grabbed her shoulders before she could hit the ground. She started to squirm and twist.

"No more fucking around," Dolph Martínez said. "Like us or not, we are the law, and we're not obliged to let ourselves be treated like this. And I'm tired of standing in the cold messing with you." He let go of her feet, and Pat Coomer let go of her shoulders. Her breath forced itself out of her mouth when she hit the ground.

They simply left her there, and whether she had no other choice or a failure of will, Sister Quinn walked to the agents and let herself be arrested.

Sister Quinn couldn't keep her teeth from chattering as she lay in the back of the Ford Bronco that the Border Patrol used to find illegal immigrants. The Border Patrol also used wire trips, sand traps that left footprints for miles, and infra-red binoculars. Still, they couldn't compete with the desperation that sent the immigrants across the border. As she shook in her light blanket, she tried to sip some of the hot coffee. It spilled out of the styrofoam cup and burned her cold hand. She rubbed at the vapor on the rear windshield and peered into the black desert, hoping to see the man who had bolted. Wounded, perhaps dying, he might be trying to get back to them. She prayed for him then fingered the vial of metallic-blue liquid in her pocket. The vial's liquid protected people.

In the front seat, Coomer and Martínez sat wrapped in blankets. Going against policy, the other agents took the illegal aliens to Alpine to be transferred to the processing center in El Paso. Martínez and Coomer would try to find the poor man who ran, then take her and him to the Presidio jail. "Hey, you want to sweeten that coffee?" Martínez asked. Sister Quinn turned her head to see Martínez reach into his jacket and pull out a pint bottle of bourbon.

"It's against regulation," Coomer said and held his cup in front of Martínez.

"Keep you warm, man," Martínez said as he poured some bourbon into Coomer's cup.

"That's a myth. Alcohol hastens freezing," Sister Quinn said,

"Yeah, well it makes me feel better," Martínez said. He knocked his knuckles against the iron mesh that separated the drivers from their outlaw passengers. "You want some?" he asked.

"No," Sister Quinn said. She pulled the blanket tighter around her and lay her head down.

"Are you warm enough?"

"Yes."

"Don't be sore," Martínez said to taunt her, then he whispered to Coomer just loud enough so that Sister Quinn could hear him: "*Pendejo curandera.*"

Cramped in the back of the Border Patrol truck,

Sister Quinn could not sleep. Every time she twisted, she woke. If she didn't twist, a foot or an arm would go to sleep. Her discomfort, though, was not pain. Pain could cleanse. It was pure. Suffering was like pain, but hard. She grunted as she felt a cramp in the arch of her foot work its way into her calf. Then, she heard a voice from the front of the truck, "Why do you do this? A judge put you on probation. And I know that the archbishop in El Paso told you to stop."

It was Pat Coomer. She whispered back, "Because these people need someone to help them."

"You're not helping them. They don't need you or want you. I've been here twelve years, same as you, and still I'm an outsider, same as you."

"Come to my church and see for yourself if I am not accepted."

"Your *templo* isn't a church. It's got nothing to do with any Catholic Church I ever knew about."

"It's the people's church."

"No, it's your church. The bishop himself would as soon close it down."

"I'd rather answer to God and that part of Him that is me than to the bishop."

"These are drug dealers, Barbara, not refugees."

"Sometimes they are the same. Maybe they were forced into this."

"Go to sleep," Coomer said.

The next morning, Sister Quinn wiped the frost from the back windshield of the truck to see that the ground was covered in about an inch of very delicate snow that looked like the crystalline ice that freezes on the top of sitting water. It made the desert look as though a sneeze could shatter the cacti, rocks, and cliffs. Sister Quinn climbed out of the back of the truck and walked to a cholla. She got down on her hands and knees and squinted at the furry spines that covered the cholla.

"*Chíngale*," she heard Coomer say behind her, "Are you praying to rocks now, *curandera*?" In a way that Coomer could never know, but maybe Martínez could know, since he had almost died here, just in looking at the snow Sister Quinn ***was*** praying to rocks.

"Let's go, Sister Quinn," she heard Pat Coomer say. But she stayed on her hands and knees and squinted to see the tiny, translucent snow banks on the spines of the cholla. She had seen snow in the desert before but had been too ignorant then to take note of it. She slowly pushed herself up and wiped at the dirt on her knees with her flat palms.

"It's snow," Martínez said. "You're a Yankee. You've seen it."

Sister Quinn climbed in the door that Martínez held open for her. She scooted to the middle of the seat, next to Pat Coomer, but still she left little room for Martínez. He pulled his shoulders close to his neck and twisted himself into the narrow space left to him. "What I wouldn't give for some *huevos* and a cup of coffee," he said.

They drove as far as they could, the truck bouncing over the rocks and screeching as cacti and creosote scratched the paint off its sides. As Dolf Martínez got out of the truck to track the signs, Pat Coomer asked Sister Quinn if she would stay in the truck, but she refused. She had training as a nurse, and the man might need some attention. So Pat Coomer and Dolf Martínez walked ahead of her, leaving tracks in the snow, while Sister Quinn waddled behind them, putting her hands on her knees to brace herself as she climbed and listened to the sound of her feet crunching the delicate layer of snow.

Soon Coomer and Martínez pointed at tiny red drops in the snow. They started to run. Sister Quinn with her girth and substance plodded behind them. She followed the trail of footprints and red dots behind a large boulder with tiny, frosted prickly pears growing out of dirt-filled indentations, and there she saw Coomer and Martínez pointing toward a body. "When the snow melts the buzzards'll come out," Dolf Martínez said.

The body was frozen. Dried, nearly black flaky blood with red speckles in it made a jagged oval on one thigh. As Sister Quinn bent closer, she saw that the wrecked container for a soul was that of a woman. Her two arms twisted up, like an ocotillo's branches, as though her last thought was to reach for help from God. Her blank face with the open mouth looked emotionless. Sister Quinn wondered if this *mojada* had prayed to Christ and Mary or had heeded the Indian genes in her *mestiza* blood and prayed to the rocks and cacti or maybe saw God take some animate form and dance in front of her.

Dolf Martínez bent over the body and yanked the woman's shirt up over her belly and stiff breasts. He laughed. Pat Coomer bent over the body and tore the package taped to her belly off the frozen woman. "Salvadoran refugee, huh?" Martínez said to Sister Quinn.

"Have you forgotten what it's like to be poor? How do you forget that you're Mexican?"

"Mexican? My name's Dolf. My father's half German. Hell, I'm a Nazi," Martínez said. "And I don't believe in all that shit, those magic cures and evil spirits." She looked at Dolf and tried to say with her eyes that she could help him with whatever evil or just simple torment was rolling around inside his head.

"How does it feel to be raped?" Pat Coomer asked her. "Whoever you're doing this for has just been using you. Now, how do you feel? Why do you do it?"

Sister Quinn didn't answer Coomer but knelt by the woman's body and prayed and wondered about this woman's suffering and soul-cleansing pain. She never finished the prayer because Coomer and Martínez grabbed the stiff body and dragged it back to the truck.

Sister Quinn drove back with Martínez and stared at the stiff body in the back of the truck. Pat Coomer followed them in Gilbert Mendoza's truck. Once they got started, Dolf stared ahead into the intense shine that snow in the desert makes and said, "In the hospital, unconscious, still holding that *curandera* charm you stuck in my hand, I had these dreams. They weren't even dreams, really. I ***felt*** myself to be a cougar. Then a desert lizard. I could feel my belly, like a lizard's, heating up from being dragged across the desert."

Sister Quinn shrugged, "People say I can fly."

"How did you know where to look for me? What were you doing up there?"

"I ***felt*** your pain." Sister Quinn smiled at Dolph. "Don't you wish you really could feel as a lizard does?"

Dolph pulled his eyes away from the rutted road to look at her and wrinkle his nose. Then, when he turned back to look at the road, with the Border Patrol truck warmed up, Sister Quinn heard one thawed arm of the woman mule hit the floor of the Texas paddy wagon.

While she sat in the Presidio County jail, the Chicano sheriff of Presidio County, Border Patrol agent Coomer, Deputy Sheriff Martínez, and a Drug Enforcement Agency officer from El Paso begged Sister Quinn to name the person who sent people across the river and the person to whom she delivered. "Maybe you don't read the papers in the ***church*** you run," Pat Coomer said, "but six illegals died in a boxcar just outside El Paso. That's the kind of people you're dealing with."

"This is a federal crime," the DEA agent said. "You can do some serious time."

Every time she shook her head or refused to name anyone, Dolf Martínez laughed at her. When everyone else was through, he asked her, "Do you really turn yourself into a *tecolote* and fly around at night?" He smiled, and held the cell door open as the others left.

She did not answer Martínez. She had gotten these people to Presidio, Marfa, or El Paso and found them decent lives. If it meant eating with the devil, she would now use a longer spoon.

By mid-afternoon, the junior pastor from St. Margaret Mary's in Presidio, Father Jesse Cordova, had the money. The bishop in El Paso had wired it to him. The cops left him alone with Sister Quinn in her cell.

Father Cordova was a young man who tried to grow a beard to look older. But he had only a few scraggly hairs on his chin and a thin moustache. He wore a down jacket over a sweat shirt, jeans, and boots. Once a month, early on Sunday morning, starting before the sun came up, he drove the St. Margaret Mary's bus to Sister Quinn's chapel and took her and some of her people to Mass at St. Margaret Mary's. Sister Quinn considered him one of her better friends.

Father Cordova hunched his shoulders, paced the cell, and said, "It's cold in here." He looked at the moisture stains in the cinder blocks. He put his hand out and pressed it against the wall to feel the cold stone.

"It will be colder in my church, Father," Sister Quinn giggled. "Three-fourths of the world shivers or sweats, most of the time."

Father Cordova looked around for a chair but saw none. Sister Quinn scooted across the rickety bunk and heard it groan from her weight. She patted the mattress next to her, but Father Cordova sat on the toilet: "You haven't stopped these cures, this hocus pocus, these half-pagan rites."

Sister Quinn put her back against the cold cinder block wall. "Did the bishop ever stop to wonder if what I do helps these people? Isn't the Marianist order devoted to healing and teaching?"

Father Cordova rested his elbows on his knees, and looked down at the floor. "Not if it is against Church doctrine."

"You know these people. You know what they believe." Sister Quinn paused, which forced Father Cordova to look up at her.

Father Cordova dropped his head to look back at the floor. "I used to know what you believed. Now, I don't. My parishioners refer to your chapel as a *templo*. They talk about your *oraciónes*. I can no longer defend you."

"So the people call my prayers *oraciónes* and my chapel a *templo*. So what? It is their church. I teach about the same God that you do."

Father Cordova rose up off the toilet and slammed his right fist into his left palm once, twice, then he shook his finger at Sister Quinn as though scolding her. "But it makes them and the Bishop think that you practice *curandos*."

Sister Quinn looked at the end of his finger and smiled. Father Cordova curled his finger back into his fist. "I thought we were interested in their souls?" Sister asked.

Father Cordova shouted, "Superstition and magic."

"Atheists think Christianity is superstition and magic," Sister Quinn said and smiled.

"Now you side with atheists," Father Cordova said quietly and hung his head.

"I've never sold them any cures. Better they come to me than to the *curanderos* in Presidio or Ojinaga. I've never taught them about miracles, except our Lord's Ascension," Sister Quinn said, then smiled inside her mind to herself over that great magical tale. If Christ could ascend, who should care if she turned into an owl?

Father Cordova straightened up and turned his back to Sister Quinn. "Okay, so you are not *curandera*. But you don't discourage unfortunate rumors. Now, a second arrest for breaking the law."

He turned to face Sister Quinn, "We are still Americans. The Church can no longer defend you." Father Cordova, Mexican and Catholic at birth, had become a Protestant. He cocked his head as though trying to understand her, "You're smiling at me."

Sister Quinn nodded.

Father Cordova dropped his head and said, "Excommunication proceedings will start." Father Cordova tried to look her in the eye. He muttered, "The bishop has written to the archbishop in San Antonio, and the archbishop agrees."

"Very well," Sister Quinn said and pushed herself up to a standing position.

Father Cordova nodded his head, "Very well then. You must first stop your practice and move into Presidio. We will then try to find a lawyer."

"No, no," Sister Quinn chuckled. "I will go on without the Church if need be."

Father Cordova's shoulders dropped. He waited, then, to his credit, found some humor: "Sister Quinn, you should have been a Marxist rather than a Catholic." Sister Quinn giggled and patted him on the shoulder. He would have been a good priest in some quiet suburban parish.

Sister Quinn's mission and home was just off what Texans called *El Camino Real*, Texas Highway 170. Nearing Big Bend National Park, the road was an engineering marvel that skirted along the sides and tops of the Texas cliffs looking down on the Río

Grande. A driver can see eagles and hawks above him and mountain goats and wild burros on both the Texas and Mexican sides if he keeps close watch and travels during the lonely times. Sister Quinn lived off in the valley between Redford and Presidio. She turned off 170 near Redford and drove down the rutted road that wound through the broad, flat fields stretching to the cane breaks at the Río Grande.

Workers in the fields were finishing planting onions. Sister Quinn liked to watch the field hands planting and harvesting the carrots, peppers, and cantaloupes. On the Mexican side, she could watch cotton pickers. On this side, just to torment the poor people, Border Patrol agents liked to drive by in their trucks to scare workers out of the fields. In the spring, at harvest time, when a Border Patrol truck would pass, someone would panic and just start running. Most of the time, farther north, no one bothered with farm workers.

With the sun setting, Sister Quinn pulled up to her ancient Volkswagen that ran only when Gilbert Mendoza ***fixed*** it. Azul, Gilbert Mendoza's runt boy, ran out of the squat room attached to the mission, and she got out of the car and hugged him. His parents called him ***Azul*** because he had been born a blue baby. She had helped deliver him along with two women from Redford and a doctor from Presidio who arrived too late to actually help with the delivery. The doctors at the clinic in Presidio said that it was a miracle he had lived. Some of Gilbert Mendoza's relatives said that it was a miracle that he had been blue. This, they were sure, was a sign from God.

With an arm around Azul, Sister Quinn walked into her hut. He had heated some *frijoles* and warmed some tortillas on Sister Quinn's old stove. The food and the stove were both from Gilbert Mendoza. To save on the electric bill, Sister Quinn and Azul shivered and ate by candlelight. These cold spells, even one as cold as this, never lasted very long. Tomorrow or the day after would be warm and dry again.

After dinner, Sister Quinn grabbed her rosary beads off the shelf in the kitchen, a candle from the kitchen table, and the dried ocotillo branch that she kept in the corner. Azul shook his head, but she said, "No, no. Come on. Don't worry," and put her arm around him and led him through the door of her hut that went into the mission.

Sister Quinn struck a match and lit the candle, which barely lit the mission, but Sister Quinn knew her cathedral well enough to make her way through it even in the dark. She walked to the railing, placed the candle on it, handed the ocotillo branch to Azul, and knelt before the crucifix and the small statue of the Virgin Mother. The flickering candle made shadows dance on the faces of Christ and Mary, emphasizing the pain and the human suffering that the Ojinaga artisan had carved into their faces.

The images of Christ and Mary hung on the front wall. On the side walls, she had hung small statuettes and pictures of saints. And whether saint or sinner, she had a reproduced photograph of Pedrito Jaramillo, the old nineteenth century *curandero*, staring out of his milky, cataract-covered eyes that didn't focus on anything. But those eyes suggested the power of his faith and his knowledge of the suffering of the world. He held his neatly folded white handkerchief, which he had used for his cures, over his heart.

Sister Quinn pulled her arms out of the sleeves of her jacket and let it fall behind her and across her calves. She slowly unclasped the first button of her blouse, then the next, and so on. She pulled her blouse below her shoulders and down to her waist. She put her elbows across the rail, pressed her breasts against the edge of it, and ran the rosary through her fingers. "*Por favor*, Azul," she said.

Sister Quinn looked back over her shoulder at Azul. He was crying. "Please, *muchacho*," she said sweetly, then turned her head to look at Christ and Mary. The ocotillo branch hit her across the shoulders, but she was almost as strong as a man, and Azul was weak. "Harder," she said and knew from the next whack that Azul had taken the ocotillo branch in both hands and swung it like a bat.

She let the rosary beads glide through her fingers and prayed to Christ and Mary. And she prayed a little bit to Jaramillo, too. And she prayed a little bit to the spirits that get into her poor people's bodies and had to be coaxed or scared out. She prayed for the wax from the candelilla plants, for the liquor from the sotol plants, and for the cures like aloe vera oil that may or may not work. "Harder," she yelled and felt the whack that would draw blood.

Sister Quinn turned to look at Azul, who held his thin, twisted, writhing baseball bat at his feet, as though preparing himself to face the next fastball, and cried. "*Pobre muchacho*," Sister Quinn cried, then said, "Harder, *por favor*." Azul wiped at his tears with the back of his hand, and Sister Quinn turned to look again at Christ and Mary and the shadows. Until she could fully feel the universal suffering of poor people and then become a part of that suffering, until she could feel adequately punished for being white and rich in a world where most were poor and dark, pain would have to do.

"Harder," she said without knowing she had said anything. The next whack across her shoulders clouded her vision. Pain gave way to numbness, and Sister Quinn wished she could feel her arms become flapping wings and be what Lupé Rodríguez wanted her to be. ■

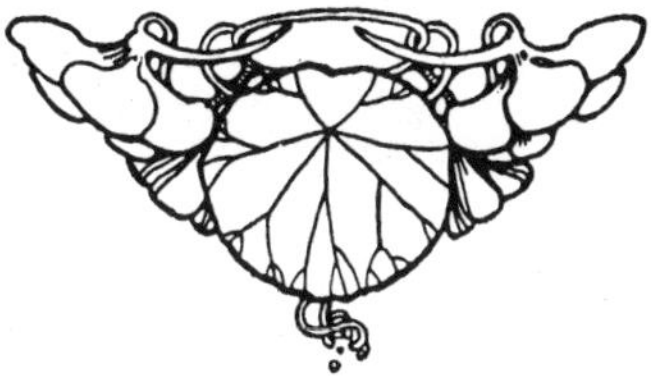